the journey:

forgiveness, restorative justice and reconciliation

Stephanie Hixon & Thomas Porter

Women's Division
The General Board of Global Ministries
The United Methodist Church

Director of Spiritual Formation and Mission Theology
Women's Division, The General Board of Global Ministries
The United Methodist Church
475 Riverside Drive, Room 1504
New York, NY 10115

All biblical quotations, unless otherwise noted, are from the New Revised Standard Version (NRSV) of the Bible, copyright © 1989 by the Division of Christian Education of the National Council of the Churches of Christ in the United States of America. Used by permission. All rights reserved.

Parts of this study have been adapted from *The Spirit and Art of Conflict Transformation, Creating a Culture of JustPeace* by Thomas Porter. © 2010 Upper Room Books®. Used by permission from Upper Room Books®. To order, phone 800-972-0433 or go to www.upperroom.org/bookstore.

The Journey: Forgiveness, Restorative Justice and Reconciliation:
ISBN: 978-1-933663-48-7
Library of Congress Control Number: 2010931736

The Journey: Forgiveness, Restorative Justice and Reconciliation (Spanish edition)
ISBN: 978-1-933663-49-4
Library of Congress Control Number: 2010931737

The Journey: Forgiveness, Restorative Justice and Reconciliation (Korean edition)
ISBN: 978-1-933663-50-0
Library of Congress Control Number: 2010931738

Printed in the United States of America

table of contents

introduction

◆ FORGIVENESS, RESTORATIVE JUSTICE AND RECONCILIATION ◆

As Christians we are called to a lifelong journey of practicing forgiveness, justice and reconciliation in our relational lives. For the first four centuries of the church's life these practices were at the heart of life in community. Before you worshipped you were asked whether you were reconciled with others.[1] The church followed Jesus' direction in the Sermon on the Mount: "So if you are offering your gift at the altar, and there remember that your brother or sister has something against you, leave your gift there before the altar and go: first be reconciled to your brother or sister, and then come and offer your gift" (Matthew 5:23-24).

The church's focus on peace and nonviolent resistance as well as the way of peace became obscured when the church became the church of the Empire in the time of Constantine. The Good News of Reconciliation and the Jesus Way is still found in the biblical story and in remarkable stories of Christians throughout the world and throughout the ages. Our hope is that the church can recover the Good News of Reconciliation as its central message and the Ministry of Reconciliation as its central practice so that every church becomes a neighborhood center, with global outreach, of forgiveness, justice and reconciliation. For us, reconciliation includes forgiveness and restorative justice. Imagine with us the difference we might make in this world if every church became a Neighborhood Reconciliation Center.

We know this is a journey, a lifelong journey of learning, trying, failing, and, yes, at times succeeding. We know how difficult this journey can be. We are all too aware of our own failures to forgive, to make right our relations and achieve reconciliation. It is a journey that involves risk: risk of failure, emotional risk and even physical risk. This is not a journey of perfection, and the journey is often messy. We believe that there is a spectrum of constructive possibilities on the journey of reconciliation, all of which should be celebrated. Like Jacob, who covenanted with his uncle Laban to guarantee each other's safety, we will find that mere coexistence is a great achievement. And, like Jacob with Esau, we hope to find those miraculous, God-filled moments when we are able to embrace and be embraced by our estranged brothers and sisters (Genesis 31-33). There is no greater moment in our lives than when such an embrace occurs. There is no moment more filled with the presence of God.

Questions for the Journey

This is a journey that we all make together. At the heart of this journey are the critical questions of our age. In our families, in our places of worship, in our communities, in our nations and in our world, we ask:

- How can we transform our conflicts into something constructive, into an opportunity for learning, growth and revelation?
- How can we live together in a way that we all will flourish?
- How can we find healing in our broken relationships?
- How can we find justice in this world, a justice that heals?
- How can we break out of the cycles of injury, retribution and violence?
- How can Christianity and all religions become a source of peace, not a source of destructive conflict?

These questions come out of experiences that many of us have had of destructive conflict, even in our families and in our churches. We have the wounds to prove it. These are questions that arise out of what has been claimed to be the most violent century the world has ever experienced and the beginning of a century that has not been the Decade to Overcome Violence, as hoped for by the World Council of Churches.[2] These are questions that become urgent when there are broken relationships, especially with those who have been close to us. We know how painful church conflicts can be, with destructive conflicts the greatest indicator of church decline.[3] We are told in the Bible that the first act of worship led to the killing of Abel by Cain (Genesis 4:8). We are more aware than ever of how religion can be a source of conflict. These are urgent questions!

For the two of us, these questions are central to one of the greatest challenges of our day, exploring the frontiers, the horizons, borders and boundaries of the relational life and working toward transforming conflicts from being destructive to being constructive. For each of us, our own journeys have led us to understand that this is the adventure and calling of the spiritual life and that the Bible is the necessary guidebook for our exploration as we engage these questions.

Our Journeys

Stephanie's Journey

During a recent worship and study time, I caught a glimpse of the book jacket on a co-worker's Bible. It read, "Warning: Reading this may be hazardous to women's emotional, physical and spiritual health." It was a bit startling but also intriguing. What was this about? Further exploration led to a heartfelt discussion of how our own biblical faith and religious traditions have at times been used to justify violence and harm toward women, children, the "other" in our midst.

As one who was birthed into, nurtured and formed in the best of Christian discipleship for people called "Methodists," I deeply love God, the church and its marvelous witness to Christ in the world. I have also grieved the ways at times that I have witnessed harm perpetrated by religious leaders and harmful practices justified by biblical passages of social order and exclusion. Howard Thurman writes about reading the Bible to his grandmother on a regular basis and how particular she was about the choice of scriptures. He finally asks her why she would not let him read any of the Pauline letters. She went on to explain that "at least three or four times a year [the minister] used as a text: 'Slaves, be obedient to them that are your master . . . as unto Christ.' Then he would go on to show how it was God's will that we were slaves and how, if we were good and happy slaves, God would bless us. I promised my Maker that if I ever learned to read and if freedom ever came, I would not read that part of the Bible." Imagine a picture of this woman of faith having a conversation with Paul when she gets to heaven. What a moment of truth-telling and reconciliation at the heavenly banquet table![4]

As a pastor, I recall the depth of pain and struggle I sensed with some in my presence — persons who had been formed in traditions that prohibited granting women authority to preach. How could I be faithful to the call to love God's own beloved, the very same with whom I experienced broken-ness? How does one conduct conversation among persons for whom "the other" calls into question one's own deeply held tenets of faith? What I learned from some of these early experiences is that while crucial, advocating for changes in social structures alone did not enable us to be reconciled. These were spiritual struggles and matters of faith; we needed to engage one another in the fullness of our faith community. The power of music, arts, shared sacraments, prayer, Bible study and authentic witness to our faith carried us through a unique and imaginative communal journey.

As an advocate for those harmed by sexual misconduct, abuse or harass-ment by religious professionals, I was keenly aware of the limitations of our church and legal systems to assist with healing, authentic accountability, justice and restoration. These retributive systems can become places where the voice and story of those harmed is disregarded and persons are dehu-manized in attempts to determine guilt or innocence.

As I reflected on these church and legal systems, my journey led to a fuller examination of the systems and processes at the heart of how we or-der our lives as United Methodists. It included a study of the significance of the Judicial Council and its authority in our faith tradition and mining the depths of my experience in both church and current Western legal practices by immersing myself in the law school study of Alternative Dispute Resolution. One colleague described the topic of my exploration as "liturgical jurisprudence." I continued to imagine the possibilities of reordering our life as a people of God to be more intentionally marked by our acts of faith and discipleship — prayer, Bible study, communing with God and one another — extending the ministry of reconciliation to the world.

In this study, we seek to explore more fully the journey of reconciliation — essentially a journey toward change that is inextricably connected to restorative justice and the gift of forgiveness.

Tom's Journey

As a trial lawyer for 25 years, I had the opportunity to see the adversarial-retributive system close up. This is a system that resolves conflicts through an adversarial process whose end result is to ascertain guilt, liability or innocence and to impose punishment or damages on those determined to be guilty or liable. As chancellor for 23 years of the New England Annual Conference of the United Methodist Church, I came to see that this system is at the heart of the way we deal with complaints or grievances in the church as well as how we deal with our theological differences. This system informs much of the decision making in the world, including the world of foreign affairs. As a lawyer trying cases both in the secular courts and in the church, I came to see the limitations and often destructive nature of this system. This system, generally, does not work to improve relationships, to resolve conflicts in a way that is healing for both parties parties, or to provide opportunities for forgiveness and reconciliation. I have spent much of my life in recent years looking for and attempting to practice a better way of dealing with conflict and harm.

In the 1990s I was first led to the study and practice of mediation. Helping people resolve their own disputes instead of fighting it out in court with someone else making the decision was like a religious experience for me.

Mediation works. Even in conflict, people can have a good conversation to get to a good place together.

In mediation, I found an alternative to the adversarial system, but I was still searching for a justice that serves this collaborative process. The answer for me came during a sabbatical studying the Truth and Reconciliation Commission in South Africa. In South Africa, Paul's image of the body of Christ came alive for me in the African understanding of *ubuntu*, which means we are who we are because of our relationships. When I dehumanize you, I dehumanize myself. We are all interconnected and interdependent. I also saw the power of the telling and hearing of stories, the practice of forgiveness, and, finally, an alternative to retributive justice in the form of restorative justice. Restorative justice insists on a collaborative engagement as the way to address the harm and needs of victims and the personal accountability of the person who did the harm so that a right relation can be established as much as possible.

In my study of restorative justice, I learned about the power of the circle process: the recognition of sacred space through ritual, the creation together of relational covenants to guide how we treat one another, the use of a talking piece to give everyone voice and promote good speaking and good listening, and a circle of collective wisdom where everyone is equally responsible for the outcome.

Our Journey

These journeys led us to work for JustPeace Center for Mediation and Conflict Transformation[5] and to the subject of this study — the journey of forgiveness, justice and reconciliation, the journey from broken relations to healing and right relations. This journey has been deeply informed by the Bible and does involve a process of spiritual formation into what Paul calls the "new creation." The bringing together of Bible study and spiritual formation describes much of what we do in our work with JustPeace, whose mission is "to assist United Methodists to engage conflict constructively in ways that strive for justice, reconciliation, resource preservation and restoration of community in the church and in the world."[6]

Recent Developments in the Study and Practice of Forgiveness, Justice and Reconciliation

We live in an age that has taken forgiveness, justice and reconciliation seriously. In 1995, Greg Jones, Dean of Duke Divinity School, published his book *Embodying Forgiveness: A Theological Analysis*, in which he noted that this "book fills a surprising void, because there have been comparatively few theological discussions of forgiveness in this century."[7] Considering how central forgiveness was to the life and teaching of Jesus, this void is striking. Much research has been done, and many books have been written in the past 20 years about forgiveness, including Bishop Tutu's book *No Future Without Forgiveness*.[8]

We also live in an age that has rediscovered restorative justice. We say *rediscovered*, as restorative justice is rooted in biblical justice and in many aboriginal justice systems throughout the world. This movement has profoundly affected the way we think about addressing harms and conflict in this world as well as how we think theologically about God's work in history. Howard Zehr, a visionary in the modern movement of restorative justice, and Barbara Toews write:

> In a mere quarter century, restorative justice has grown from a few scattered experimental projects into a social movement, and then into an identifiable field of practice and study. Moving out from its origins within the criminal justice arena, restorative justice is being applied in schools, in homes, and in the workplace. Restorative justice approaches and concepts are being used to address issues on the micro level — among individuals, within communities — but, as illustrated by South Africa's Truth and Reconciliation Commission, are also being applied to the macro level.[9]

We have also found that beliefs and practices of retributive justice (which simply asks whether you did it, and, if so, how you should be punished) block the work of forgiveness and reconciliation, whereas restorative justice provides a context and way that is conducive to the experience of forgiveness and reconciliation. Reconciliation assumes "right relations," "just relations." How we understand justice is critical to how we understand and experience reconciliation.

Robert Schreiter, one of the most profound students of reconciliation, has noted that since the fall of the Berlin wall in 1989, there has been a focus on reconciliation both in the theological and political realms, with the most notable example being the Truth and Reconciliation Commission in South Africa.[10] The United Nations designated 2009 as the International Year of Reconciliation.

We believe that we are part of a movement rediscovering the Good News of Reconciliation as the central message of the Christian faith and seeing the call to be reconcilers at the heart of our self-understanding of what it means to be people of faith. We do find, as we have noted earlier, that the understanding of reconciliation includes forgiveness and restorative justice.

Bible Study as a Transforming and Reconciling Experience

We are delighted to write a Bible study. In our work of conflict transformation, we have found the Bible to be our key text. Much of what we have learned from the secular study of mediation, restorative justice and peace building is found in a most profound way in the Bible. The Bible teaches primarily through stories. We have found that the telling and hearing of stories is at the heart of our work. Moreover, we believe that learning about the relational life and developing relational skills takes place in community. We learn from one another whenever we come together. Studying from the one text — the one document — is a powerful way to learn from one another, to hear one another's stories, to develop community and new relations: in short, to have a transforming and reconciling experience. In communal Bible study, we can encounter the spirit of Pentecost, the spirit of God, and the creation of community in the midst of difference.

The Bible is not a book just understood by the "experts." While experts can help illumine aspects of the study of the Bible, we believe that the scripture was written for the whole people of God. One of the goals of this study is to affirm everyone's "own critical capacities, their own intellectual depth, and the right and ability to think for themselves."[11]

We do have some reflections to share, but these are offered only after each person has engaged the text directly with fresh eyes, ears and heart, making notes of their own observations and questions, finding their own voice and wisdom. Everyone will have the opportunity to make connections between the text and their own experience before hearing what connections are made by others. This time of personal reflection will involve both intellectual and personal encounter. Then the sharing of these reflections along with our reflections will, we hope, generate even more understanding of the truths that the text offers us in our own journey and in our communal journey of forgiveness, justice and reconciliation. Together we will discover insights none of us had before we entered into the study together.

Bible study is not group therapy or just a comfortable time together but a community experience where each person feels free to be and become themselves in community. Our goal for ourselves in this study is both personal and social transformation, not just receiving information. On this journey we hope that each one of us can discover our unique gifts for the ministry of reconciliation and our own way toward forgiveness, justice and reconciliation in our own relations. We also hope that together we can see ways of finding forgiveness, justice and reconciliation within the larger social order, understanding how systems and structures violate people's lives and how these structures can be transformed to be more just and more conducive to human and cosmic well-being.

The Journey, the Worldview and the Practice

We are going to begin this Bible study in Chapter 1 with the real-life journey of Jacob as found in Genesis 32-33. Jacob is a human being who is flawed, imaginative, deceptive, bold and offending. He is also led by God as he wrestles with God and experiences a covenant of safety with Laban and reconciliation with his brother Esau. We have found the journey of Jacob in dealing with Laban and with his brother Esau very realistic, instructive, comforting and inspiring.

In Chapter 2, we will turn to the foundational texts of the Christian life. First, we will study the Great Commandment to love God, neighbor and self, the sum of the Law and the Prophets (Matthew 22:37-39). Then we will study Paul's summary of his theology of reconciliation (2 Corinthians 5:16-20), which recognizes God's initiative in reconciling with us in spite of our failure to love, and God's call to us to be ministers of reconciliation. The biblical worldview, as seen in these scriptures, is relational. God is a relational God of love who has created a relational world. It's all about relationships. In a world that lives out of a worldview of the autonomous individual, we need to understand that the reality of the created order is relational. Understanding and being grounded in this reality is essential to the work of forgiveness, justice and reconciliation.

We know we should love God, neighbor and self. We know that we fail to do so and need to be reconciled and to be reconcilers. But how do we practice forgiveness, restorative justice and reconciliation? In Chapter 3, we study Matthew 18 where Jesus offers very practical guidance. Here Jesus shares with us lessons that the fields of conflict transformation and restorative justice have relearned in recent history. Matthew 18 begins and ends with two of the greatest sources of conflict and violence: power and money. The chapter begins with the question from the disciples of Jesus: "Who is the greatest in the kingdom of heaven?" It ends with the issue of the forgiveness of debt. One whose debt is bigger than all the debt of Mesopotamia is forgiven. This debtor then turns on his small debtor, throws him into jail, and subsequently suffers the consequences of one who is forgiven but does not forgive. In between, we are given

- an analysis as to why we have destructive conflict and violence — the problems created by trying to be greater than another;
- an understanding that God is present with us in the midst of conflict;
- an understanding of why Jesus calls us to be "like a child" and of what it means to say peacemakers are children of God;

- practical advice on how to deal with conflict and harm: the journey of reconciliation, the journey of restorative justice;
- the story of the lost sheep with its vision of no one being lost and the celebration that occurs when restoration of relationship takes place;
- the radical breaking of cycles of woundedness, retribution and violence through the act of forgiveness; and
- an understanding of the deep reality of creation, seeing the consequences of not following the path of reconciliation and restorative justice, being told that if we do not forgive we will not be able to experience forgiveness, and if we do not follow the journey of responding to those we have harmed we will not be able to experience the Kingdom.

Key Guideposts on the Journey

We understand from Matthew 18 that the person harmed should go directly to the person who has done the harm. In many situations of deep harm, we know this can be difficult. How can the person harmed and living through trauma seek such an engagement? Whether experiencing harm and brokenness personally or communally, in Chapters 4, 5, 6 and 7 we look more deeply into the experience of being harmed, doing harm and moving toward forgiveness, justice and reconciliation.

In Chapter 4 we explore the importance of grieving and confronting our fears. Themes of lament run deeply throughout the biblical witness, and we will pause in the place of Holy Saturday, with the women at the foot of the cross. Allowing ourselves to grieve and mourn the harm we've experienced is a critical first step in our healing and reconciling journey. Naming our fears is essential to being able to deprive our fears of their power and to enable us to see them as challenges, not crippling realities. From the place of Holy Saturday, we are invited to imagine more fully the grace of the resurrection, with the women at the empty tomb.

The journey of reconciliation is also marked by truth-telling. In Chapter 5 we seek ways to find our voice in naming our truth, telling our stories and confronting that which has harmed us and left us estranged. Jesus himself is found at the frontier, the border of a new reality in his encounter with the Canaanite Woman (Matthew 15). We complete the chapter with a closer look at the radical act of Jesus naming the truth of betrayal and yet offering bread not a stone at the Last Supper (Mark 14).

The practice of forgiveness is at the heart of our faith — both gift and choice. We will plumb the depths of the experience of the Prodigal (Luke 15) in Chapter 6. Repentance and restitution are critical and authentic aspects of a journey toward reconciliation, justice and forgiveness. How do Zacchaeus, Abigail and David illumine the path of "making things right?" We will explore this and elements of restorative justice in Chapter 7.

This journey of reconciliation is by no means linear, neat or the same for every individual or community. These guideposts provide a place from which to explore elements of faith and scripture at the heart of our Christian witness and experience of forgiveness, justice and reconciliation.

Interfaith Reconciliation

In Chapter 8 we study how Paul, Peter, James and the early church came to understand the message and the spirit of Jesus as they addressed the hostility between Jews and Gentiles in the early Christian community. In Acts 15, the story of the Jerusalem Council, we see how they came to consensus after much debate about the inclusion of the Gentiles. This remarkable story, we believe, can guide us in the work of interfaith relations. As Hans Küng has pointed out, there will be no peace in the world without peace

Four Session Study

This book is written for eight sessions of two hours each. The book can also be used with four sessions. We would suggest that everyone read the whole book, but, if you can do only four sessions, study together the chapters in the following sequence:

1. Chapter 1
2. Chapter 4
3. Chapter 5
4. Chapter 6

If you can study only one session, we suggest Chapter 1.

between our religions.[12] Making this peace is one of the critical challenges of our day. We have a witness in Acts 15 that can guide us.

Preparation for the Study

Both leaders and participants will prepare for this study in the same way. We all have the ability to both participate in and lead these sessions.

- First, read the text over several times, reading the text as if for the first time. Approach the text with deep curiosity, suspending your assumptions that you know what it means. Be prepared to discover truths that previous generations, living out of a different context, were not able to see.
- Then spend some time writing down your thoughts and your questions, re-reading the text, and going deeper in your own reflections. Write down all of your thoughts and questions. Don't censor any question. Put these reflections and questions in a journal that you will keep throughout the study.
- After spending some time with the text and your own reflections and questions, read our questions. Engage the questions we have asked, continuing to write in your journal.
- After living with the text, your thoughts and questions read the reflections we have written, which we hope will encourage a dialogue and lead to further ideas and questions. Continue to write your thoughts and questions in your journal.
- Before coming to the study, pray your questions and pray for openness to the Holy Spirit as the Holy Spirit speaks through others in the group.

As leaders, further preparation is described on pages 15-21, "The Rhythms of the Bible Study Circle."

The Circle Process: Creating Space for Encountering God, the Biblical Text and One Another

In this Bible Study, you will have the opportunity to experience the circle process. In our work of conflict transformation, we find this to be the most powerful process for providing a space where people, even in conflict, can have a good conversation to get to a good place together. It provides a space safe enough for the telling and hearing of stories, opening up our own stories in response to the text. The circle process takes place in a circle of chairs, ideally with six to 10 people. We understand that in large groups you may have more than one circle. Multiple circles will allow greater contribution from each person and will allow more than one person the opportunity to facilitate a circle. In the image of the circle you have a visual representation of our interconnection and interdependence. In the circle, everyone is equal, each being the alpha and omega of the circle. We each take responsibility for adding our wisdom to the conversation and hearing the wisdom of others. In a circle process everyone's voice is heard.

The circle is a sacred space where God's presence is recognized with an opening and closing ritual. Together the group determines a relational covenant as to how each member of the group will be treated. The work of the group is framed by questions that take the group together deeper and deeper into the text and their own experience. In the beginning a talking piece is used to make sure that every voice is heard.[13]

Conclusion

We believe that "The Journey" for all Christians is the journey of forgiveness, justice and reconciliation. We believe that the whole world is groaning to see the practice, not just the talk. Jesus knew that this journey was "The Way" out of the cycles of woundedness, retribution and violence. The future of the creation depends on our following this way. Thank God we have God's presence and power working for *shalom*, right relations and reconciliation. Thank God we have God's Word to guide us. The Bible is the essential guidebook for this journey. There is nothing more helpful or exciting than studying this guidebook together in community. We are honored that you have joined us on this journey and the experience of personal and social transformation as we learn together how to practice forgiveness, justice and reconciliation.

◆ THE LEADER'S ADDITIONAL PREPARATION ◆

As we mentioned previously in the introduction, all have the ability to both participate in and lead these sessions. We invite all of you to read this additional information on leading the Bible Study Circle.

The Rhythms of the Bible Study Circle

ENCOUNTERING GOD

The Circle begins with a centering ritual, recognizing that we are in the presence of God and that we will be guided by the Holy Spirit. We are suggesting that you place a small round worship table at the center of the Circle that can hold different objects and symbols forming part of the ritual life of the Circle. As the leader, you will have the responsibility of guiding what is placed on the table. You can invite people to bring objects for the table. You will also prepare the opening ritual. In the ritual, we open ourselves to God as well as to one another. We will provide examples that you can use in each session. You will also prepare a closing ritual that recognizes the guidance of the Spirit as well as the wisdom of the group, as everyone goes forth from leaning into the text to living the text.

ENGAGING ONE ANOTHER

At the first session of the Bible Study the group will affirm a relational covenant as to how each member of the group is to be treated in the conversation. We have found in our work that there is nothing more powerful in preventing destructive conflict than such a relational covenant. In the Bible, covenants define the life of God with God's creation as well as between human beings. These covenants recognize how we want to be treated in our life and study together and express mutual accountability and responsibility for being faithful to the covenant. We are suggesting that the following covenant be considered and adapted by each group to serve its own purposes.

OUR COVENANT

We covenant to:

Prepare prayerfully and carefully for the study.

Speak with respect.

- When the talking piece is being used, speak only when holding the talking piece.
- Be honest — saying what you think, not what you think you should say.
- Speak only for yourself.
- Speak in a way that encourages dialogue.
- Be brief and to the point.

Listen with respect.

- Listen for understanding the text and one another.
- Try to understand perspectives that differ from yours and respect the fact that the goal is not consensus on the meaning of a text but learning and sharing.
- Carefully hold all the differences together.
- Be open to new viewpoints, new ideas — to being transformed.

Keep confidential those personal stories shared in the Circle.

Stay in the Circle throughout the discussion and come to all of the sessions, if at all possible.

Each group can consider whether there are additions or changes to this covenant. What is important is that the group support this covenant after all changes and additions are made by consensus. The covenant should be posted in the room and reaffirmed at the beginning of each session.

Engaging the Text[14]

QUESTIONS AND CONVERSATION

The engagement of the text begins with the reading of the text out loud. Ask for a volunteer or volunteers to read the text. Prior to the study each participant will have read the text and formulated questions and responses in a journal. Each participant will have read our Reflection, followed by further responses and questions recorded in the journal. All of this will be assumed as the group turns directly from the reading to the questions for each session, with additional questions added by the group.

The leader will ask the first question and then give the talking piece to the person on the left to respond to the question. The talking piece will then go person to person around the Circle, with each person responding to the question until it comes back to the leader. The person holding the talking piece gets to speak without interruption, and everyone else gets to listen. A person can pass for whatever reason. The talking piece can be anything that is respected by the group. Some suggestions: a Bible, a shell, the covenant wrapped up as a scroll, a feather or a compass. We make recommendations for each session. The only limitation in choosing the talking piece is your imagination and the approval of the group. After the first round on the first question, you might, as the leader, hold the talking piece and open the group for conversation on this question with the understanding that participants do not interrupt while someone is speaking. The covenant includes an agreement by the participants to be brief and to the point out of respect for each person's right to speak. Then when you ask the second question, you can use the talking piece again to make sure that all voices are being heard as each person responds to the second question.

The focus before the exercise in each session is on the questions and on a good conversation about the text. After you have dealt with your questions, you can open the group to conversation around other questions that come from the group. The Reflection will inform the discussion as everyone will have read it, but it is not read again in the context of the group, unless someone wants to refer to it. You can refer to it in your questions.

Formulating questions is the most important task of the leader as well as the participants. T.S. Eliot described Jesus as one who knew how to ask questions.[15] Much of what Jesus says is in the form of a question. Rainer Maria Rilke has helped us understand the importance of questions and the power of living with the questions, saying,

> Be patient toward all that is unsolved in
> your heart and try to love the questions
> themselves like locked rooms and like books
> that are written in a very foreign tongue. Do
> not now seek the answers, which cannot be
> given you because you would not be able to
> live them. And the point is to live everything.
> Live the questions now.[16]

Living the question is more about finding inspiration than answers. This is consistent with what Jung said about growing not from a problem but from a more compelling life force.[17]

Elie Wiesel takes the asking of questions to a higher level in *Night*, his memoir about the Holocaust. As a young man, Wiesel's spiritual master, Moche, tells him that every question possesses a power that does not lie in its answer. The two men then engage in a discussion about the relationship between humankind and God, and the power of questions in moving toward God. Moche adds that he cannot understand God's answers to his prayers. Wiesel then asks Moche why, then, does he pray? Moche replies, "I pray to the God within me that He will give me the strength to ask Him the right questions."[18] Whether asking questions of God or of participants in a circle, our prayer is to ask good questions.

In formulating questions, be as simple and clear as possible, starting with questions related to the data easily identified in the text. Refrain from asking questions that can be answered "yes" or "no." Such questions are often techniques of cross-examination in the courtroom. Bible study is not a place for cross-examination. In short, don't ask questions that are intended to elicit right answers. Ask open-ended questions that open up both thoughts and feelings. Don't be afraid of emotions. In the process, trust your questions. Integrate other questions as they arise, but keep the structure and sequence of your questions. Be comfortable with silence. Don't break the silence with your own answer. Turn statements that you would like to make into questions. Ask questions that open up people's best experiences, their hopes, their dreams. The circle will become a spiral as you go deeper and deeper into the text.

As the leader you set the tone of respect that honors each participant. The most important preparation is to refrain from the need to control or the need to have the right answer, remembering that your role is to create the space where people can learn together, tell their own stories and find and share their own wisdom.

The process of going deeper into the text and into the depth of our experience is a rich source of learning and spiritual growth. It may be helpful to prepare for potentially deep conversation from the beginning. When discussing the covenant, the leader can acknowledge that each one enters the Circle and study voluntarily. Remind participants that the discussion may tap into areas of pain and trauma.

Prior to the start of your session, identify persons and resources available to members of the study for pastoral care and support. As participants, you are responsible to care for yourself and your participation. As leaders, you are responsible to be stewards of the process. Invite persons to take responsibility for their own participation. For example, it is appropriate for a member of the group to pass the talking stick if he or she feels more comfortable doing so.

Exercises

"It is a curious fact," says Walter Wink, "that the most revelatory insights have most often come to people, not during the more intellectual discussion of the text, but in the application exercises, when they were painting, dialoguing or working with clay."[19] This brings us to the exercises. We find this potentially the most profound experience in the study. Wink asserts that Bible study often only involves the left brain and leaves out the right brain. The left hemisphere dominates the right side of the body and normally specializes in temporal and causal relations, speech, logic, analysis, verbal behavior, abstract thinking. The right hemisphere dominates the left side and handles spatial relations, gestalts, synthesis of the whole, the grasping of meaning-in-context, which is synthetic, metaphorical, imaginative and holistic. The right side is seen most fully in artists of all kinds. Metaphors, word pictures and parables come from the right brain and must be grasped by the right brain. We believe with Wink that we need in our study to integrate the left and right brain so that the text becomes incarnate, felt and lived.

So we turn from questions and conversation to exercises that bring the whole self to the text. We have made suggestions for such exercises in each chapter. Each of these exercises is designed to bring our creativity and imagination to the text. We invite you to think of more options. The exercise should be integrally related to the central thrust of the text, not just a human relations exercise tacked onto the study.

Closing Ritual

After all of the conversations and the completion of the exercises, you will then lead the group in a closing ritual that recognizes the guidance of the Holy Spirit and the contributions of the participants to the learning of the group.

Notes

1. Willard M. Swartley, *Covenant of Peace: The Missing Peace in New Testament Theology and Ethics* (Cambridge, U.K.: William B. Eerdmans Publishing Co., 2006), pp. 185-188.

2. The WCC has worked to call attention to the role of the churches both as implicated in violence as well as forces for its transformation.

3. C. Kirk Hadaway, *FACTS on Growth: A New Look at the Dynamics of Growth and Decline in American Congregations Based on the Faith Communities Today 2005 National Survey of Congregations* (Hartford: Faith Communities Today and CCSP, 2007), p. 16.

4. Renita J. Weems, "Reading Her Way through the Struggle: African American Women and the Bible," *Stony the Road We Trod: African American Biblical Interpretation.* Cain Hope Felder, ed.,

(Minneapolis: Augsburg/Fortress Press, 1991), pp. 57-77. Ms. Weems takes this anecdote from *Jesus and the Disinherited* by Howard Thurman, published by Abingdon Press in 1949.

5. www.justpeaceumc.org.

6. Paragraph 2406, *The 2008 Book of Discipline of The United Methodist Church* (Nashville: The United Methodist Publishing House, 2008), p. 701.

7. L. Gregory Jones, *Embodying Forgiveness: A Theological Analysis* (Grand Rapids: Wm. B. Eerdmans Publishing Co., 1995), p. xiii.

8. Desmond Mpilo Tutu, *No Future Without Forgiveness* (New York: Image, Doubleday, 1999).

9. Howard Zehr and Barb Toews, eds., *Critical Issues in Restorative Justice* (Monsey, N.Y.: Criminal Justice Press, 2004), p. vii. See also Appendix A.

10. Robert Schreiter, "The Road to Reconciliation." Lecture, Symposium at Boston College School of Theology and Ministry, Boston, April 16, 2009.

11. Walter Wink, *Transforming Bible Study: A Leader's Guide* (Nashville: Abingdon Press, 1980), p. 103.

12. Hans Küng, *Global Responsibility, In Search of New World Ethic* (New York: Crossroad, 1991), p. xv.

13. For an in-depth discussion of the circle process, see Thomas Porter, *The Spirit and Art of Conflict Transformation, Creating a Culture of JustPeace* (Nashville: Upper Room Books, 2010), p. 75.

14. We recommend for additional reading Walter Wink's books, *The Bible in Human Transformation* (Philadelphia: Fortress Press, 1973) and *Transforming Bible Study, A Leader's Guide* (Nashville: Abingdon Press, 1980).

15. T. S. Eliot, "Choruses from The Rock," 1934.

16. Rainer Maria Rilke, *Letters to a Young Poet* (New York: W.W. Norton, 1954), pp. 34-35.

17. Diana Whitney, Claudia Liebler and David Cooperrider, "Appreciative Inquiry in Organizations and International Development: An Invitation to Share and Learn Across Fields," in *Positive Approaches to Peacebuilding*, eds. Cynthia Sampson, Mohammed Abu-Nimer, Claudia Liebler and Diana Whitney (Washington, D.C.: Pact Publications, 2003), p. 27.

18. Elie Wiesel, *Night* (New York: Avon Books, 1958), p. 14.

19. Walter Wink, *Transforming Bible Study: A Leader's Guide* (Nashville: Abingdon Press), p. 109.

the journey, the worldview
and the practice

Chapter 1

the real-life journey of Jacob

But Esau ran to meet him, and embraced him, and fell on his neck and kissed him, and they wept. — Genesis 33:4

Preparation

Read the whole of Jacob's journey (Genesis 25-33) as you prepare for this session. The session will focus primarily on Chapters 32 and 33, but the whole story is as intriguing a story as any you have ever read, and it is important to see the whole of this journey of reconciliation, including the estrangement.

- Keep a notebook or journal to record questions, insights and reflections as you prepare for the study and to keep notes in during and after the class.

- List all of the questions you have about the texts. Spend time letting these questions form and go deeper and deeper. Note your insights.

- Look at the questions we have asked and write down your thoughts as to where these questions lead you, which includes other questions.

- Spend some time with the text and your journaling before you turn to the reflections that follow.

- After you have read the Reflection section, write down in your journal other insights and questions you have.

Setup

A small round table is in the middle of the room, as a worship center, with a circle of chairs surrounding the table at a comfortable distance. On the table is a single candle, symbolizing our search for the Light in the scriptures and symbolizing our unity in Christ. Some light refreshments are in the room. Place on the table a map and a compass. Consider using the compass as a talking piece, a symbol for the journey.

Centering

The leader welcomes everyone as the candle is lighted.

Prayer

The leader leads a prayer that everyone says together.

> Loving and Persistent God, you do not give up on us. As the one who wrestles with us through the night and brings us to the dawn of enlightenment, we seek your presence and illumination for this study.
>
> Open us to your wisdom and insight as we seek to understand one another's perspective. Open us to your love and to one another as we yearn to open walls that divide us. Open us to the transforming power of your Spirit and grant us courage, patience and determination for the ministry of reconciliation. Amen.

Hymn

"Jesus, Lover of My Soul"   **(UMH#479)**
or "Stand By Me"   **(UMH#512)**

Introductions

The compass is described and consensus is tested on using it as a talking piece. Using the talking piece, everyone introduces herself or himself and describes why this study of forgiveness, restorative justice and reconciliation is of interest or importance to them. The talking piece is passed around the Circle from left to right as each person speaks.

Relational Covenant

In the Bible, covenants play an essential role, such as in the relationship between God and Israel and between human beings in a variety of settings. Covenants recognize the relationship and express the mutual responsibilities of those who are party to the covenant.

In our life together, in our churches, nothing is more helpful in preventing destructive conflict than a covenant as to how we are to be treated in community, how members of the Body of Christ are to be treated.

The following covenant for our conversation is merely a starting point for developing your own covenant:

OUR COVENANT

We covenant to:

Prepare prayerfully and carefully for the study.

Speak with respect.
- When the talking piece is being used, speak only when holding the talking piece.
- Be honest — saying what you think, not what you think you should say.
- Speak only for yourself.
- Speak in a way that encourages dialogue.
- Be brief and to the point.

Listen with respect.
- Listen for understanding the text and one another.
- Try to understand opinions that differ from yours and respect the fact that the goal is not consensus on the meaning of a text but learning and sharing.

- Carefully hold all the differences together.
- Be open to new viewpoints, new ideas — to being transformed.

Keep confidential those personal stories shared in the Circle.

Stay in the Circle throughout the discussion and come to all of the sessions, if at all possible.

Ask if there are changes or additions that the group would make to this covenant. A discussion follows of any changes or additions, with these changes or additions made by consensus. You will find that people are generally willing to live with the covenant provided here with few changes, but it is important that the covenant be one that is owned and supported by the participants. After discussion and consensus on changes or additions, ask if the covenant is one that everyone will support in the study together.

The covenant should then be posted in the room where everyone can see it.

Reading of the Text

Since everyone has read Genesis 32-33, we suggest that you ask a volunteer or volunteers to read Genesis 32:3-8, 32:22-30 and 33:1-11 in the NRSV. After the reading, go directly to the discussion of the questions.

Questions

Leader: What follows are just some suggested questions to help you formulate questions for group discussion. We would suggest having four or five questions prepared. Others will flow from the conversation. After each question you ask, use the talking piece passed around the Circle to the left, to hear all of the voices as participants respond to the question. After everyone has been heard, hold the talking piece so that the conversation can flow naturally, building on what has been said. When you get to the second question, follow the same practice with the talking piece. Save 30 minutes at the end for the exercise and the concluding ritual.

- What are the different steps Jacob takes to find favor with Esau? Are these steps different from ones you have taken in reestablishing estranged relationships?
- Who does Jacob struggle with during the night? God? An angel? Esau? Himself? With what or with whom do you struggle?
- Jacob receives both a wound — a dislocated hip — and a new identity in the struggle. What is going on here? Have you had a similar experience?
- Jacob's journey included pleas from his mother Rebecca to flee for safety and hopes for distance and forgetting. What do you imagine as Esau's journey that brought Esau from wanting to kill his brother to running to embrace him?
- What does Jacob mean when he says that seeing Esau's face is like seeing the face of God?
- What promise do you see today for all of the descendants of Jacob and Esau overcoming their differences?

REFLECTION THE REAL-LIFE JOURNEY OF JACOB

The reflections in this study are to stimulate your own thinking, finding what is meaningful to you in the passage. They are not intended to limit possible interpretations of the text.

An Overview of the Journey

In this section, we will discuss, as background to the scripture we are studying, Jacob's journey prior to his journey back from the land of Laban to meet Esau.

RECONCILIATION IS A JOURNEY

The story of Jacob begins with the estrangement from Esau, as Jacob exploits Esau to get his birthright for a bowl of lentil stew and then lies to his blind father to steal the blessing. Jacob has to flee as Esau swore to kill him, traveling 400 miles to find a wife and sojourn with Laban. Here Jacob finds himself in conflict with Laban, ultimately flees and is chased by Laban as he tries to return to the land of Esau, his homeland. With Laban he avoids bloodshed by entering into a covenant of coexistence and then avoids bloodshed with Esau as Esau embraces him. Jacob is literally on a physical journey, but the journey is primarily a spiritual journey. On his travels he has two defining encounters with God, one as he is fleeing and one as he is returning. As with many journeys of reconciliation, Jacob is wrestling with God, with Esau and with himself.

Reconciliation is a Very Human Journey

There is hope for all of us in the story of Jacob. In the story of Jacob, we see our dilemmas and aspects of our selves: sibling rivalry, family problems, coveting and calculation, exploitation, manipulation, lies, anger and grief. If God can journey with the likes of Jacob on the road to reconciliation, God can journey with us. Walter Brueggemann states in his study of Genesis, which has informed our reflection, "The narrative exemplifies what is generally true of Genesis. This is not a spiritual treatise on morality. It is rather, a memory of how faith moves in the rawness of experience."[20]

We see that reconciliation takes place in the midst of a life of conflict, conflict with his brother, his father, his father-in-law, with God and even his beloved Rachel concerning whose fault it was that they had no child. We all know how destructive conflict can be, and we see this in the life of Jacob. We see in this story the web of human relations in which we all live and how the actions of one can affect the lives of all. We also know that conflict is a natural part of life, even necessary, and does not need to be destructive. There is great hope for all of us in our own conflicts in seeing that even the highly conflicted Jacob can find peace with his father-in-law and reconciliation with his brother.

Reconciliation is a Journey with God

God is intertwined with these human relations and in these conflicts that we address theologically and biblically in Chapters 2 and 3. God pronounces, "Two nations are in your womb, and two peoples born of you shall be divided; one shall be stronger than the other, the elder shall serve the younger" (Genesis 25:23).

Here God is challenging the system of primogeniture, a very old law (Deuteronomy 21:15-17). Primogeniture created an orderly way of passing on rights and privileges, but it advantaged the firstborn to the detriment of the younger son. The oldest son inherited the estate. The entire Genesis account with Jacob and Esau is a challenge to this whole system. And, even though women were not portrayed with much public power, rights or privileges in the Genesis accounts, Susan Fiditch reminds us that "the God of Genesis, with whom the important value judgment lies, is partial to marginal people of both genders."[21]

The conflict with Esau flows from this change in the power relations pronounced by God and obtained by Jacob through exploitation and lies. It is interesting to note that Esau is never ruled by Jacob. The deception leads to 20 years of exile for Jacob and loneliness for Rebecca, who never sees her son again. Jacob, who becomes known as Israel, does finally realize the promises God made to him as he ends his journey by returning to Canaan. Both Esau and Jacob flourish.

Jacob meets God twice in the night on his journey, once in the vision at Bethel and then at the wrestling encounter at Penuel. God is present in the midst of conflict, a reality that we will encounter in the biblical texts throughout this study. The stories of the human conflicts and of the encounters with God cannot be separated from each other in Jacob's journey or in our journey.[22]

We will discuss the encounter at Penuel later. At Bethel God affirms the promises made to the patriarchs of land and offspring and the promise of well-being that will come to others because of Israel. God then goes on to make three promises for the journey to Jacob: "Know that I am with you and will keep you wherever you go, and will bring you back to this land" (Genesis 28:15).

The first promise is the promise of accompaniment or presence — "I am with you." Here we find a central text of the Bible. For example, in Joshua, "Be strong and courageous; do not be frightened or dismayed, for the LORD your God is with you wherever you go" (Joshua 1:9). Jesus at his birth is called "Emmanuel, which means 'God with us'" (Matthew 1:23). God promises to be always present.

The second promise is protection: to "keep you wherever you go." God will actively protect Jacob from harm. God is the shepherd who will care for his sheep. In Chapter 3 we will deal with the story of the lost sheep and the promise that God does not want anyone to be lost (Matthew 18:12-14).

The third promise is the promise that God will bring Jacob home, "back to the land." We can come home, no matter how far we stray. We will explore this more when we discuss the story of the Prodigal in Chapter 6.

The promises of presence, protection and homecoming are promises sufficient for any journey.

It's a Journey with a Spectrum of Possibilities

We know that the type of reconciliation that Jacob achieves with Esau is not the end story of every journey of dealing with harm and conflict. The story of Jacob and Laban, which ends in a covenant of coexistence, shows us that something short of reconciliation should be honored and celebrated on this journey.

In Laban, Jacob met his match in deception and guile. Jacob was told by Laban that he would receive his love, Rachel, in marriage after seven years of service. Jacob finished the task, but, under cover of darkness, Laban brought his eldest daughter Leah to Jacob. Jacob had to work another seven years for the woman he loved. Laban's rationale for his deception was that custom required him to give the firstborn instead of the younger. Here again we see the system of primogeniture.

Jacob also noted that Laban had changed his wages 10 times. In short, there was great conflict between the son-in-law and the father-in-law.

Then Jacob heard what Laban's sons were saying about him and saw that

Laban no longer favored him. God told Jacob to leave and return to his land. Jacob outwitted Laban, not telling him he was going to leave. Three days later Laban learned about Jacob's flight and pursued Jacob. He pursued him for seven days, and Jacob feared there would be a violent end to this pursuit.

God intervened again on behalf of Jacob and told Laban, "Take heed that you say not a word to Jacob, either good or bad" (Genesis 31:24). Jacob and Laban then came to a remarkable covenant. They built two pillars to each of their gods and guaranteed each other safety: "The Lord watch between you and me, when we are absent one from the other" (Genesis 31:49). They did not embrace, as Esau and Jacob did, but they worked out a covenant of coexistence. This would be a remarkable achievement in Israel and Palestine, or in Iraq today. The image of the recognition of the God of Abraham and the God of Nahor might also be a guide for, at least, coexistence among the world religions, as we will discuss later in Chapter 8.

As a journey, there is no one script for everyone. It is seldom a step-by-step process. Every journey is different. The journey takes time, and all persons must be patient with themselves and follow their own pace.

The Journey of Jacob to Esau

Now we return to the conflict with Esau. The last we saw of Esau he vowed to kill Jacob. Jacob fled to avoid another fratricide such as Cain's killing of Abel. Twenty years later, Jacob returns to meet Esau. Genesis Chapter 32 begins with the presence of angels, recognizing God is keeping the promises made at Bethel. The presence of angels does not stop Jacob from doing everything he can to control the situation, nor does it stop him from being "greatly afraid and distressed" (Genesis 32:7). Angels are often present in biblical stories of encounters with the holy. In Chapter 4 we explore the experience of the women at the tomb and the comforting words of the angel, "Be not afraid."

THE JOURNEY INVOLVES RISK, ANXIETY AND FEAR
For all Jacob knows, Esau still wants to kill him. In returning, there is

this risk. He sends messengers, only to learn that Esau is coming with 400 men. In fear and distress, Jacob divides up his people and animals into two companies, hoping that one will escape if the other is destroyed. The night before the engagement, he sent his two wives, his two maids and his 11 children across the Jabbok. He stays back. Then after his nightlong struggle, which included a struggle with his own fear and anxiety, he did go ahead of his family, putting them in danger in the reverse order of his affection for them, with the maids and their children first, Leah and her children second, and with Rachel and Joseph at the back. We discuss the importance of naming our fears in Chapter 4.

THE JOURNEY INVOLVES PLANNING

Jacob first sent messengers to Esau with a message that sounds like that of a victim, "I have lived with Laban as an alien, and stayed until now." He then tries to impress with his prosperity, and, finally, seeks favor in the sight of Esau (Genesis 32:3-5). There is no apology. The result of this message was heightened anxiety over knowledge that Esau was coming to him with 400 men.

Then Jacob tries gifts. He sends waves of gifts to Esau, with the message that they are presents "sent to my lord Esau" (Genesis 32:18). With the birthright and the blessing, Jacob is Lord over Esau, but, in this reversal, Jacob addresses Esau as Lord. He describes his motivation, "For he thought, 'I may appease him with the present that goes ahead of me, and afterwards I shall see his face; perhaps he will accept me'" (Genesis 32:20). Brueggemann says that the word for appease is *kpr*, and that "the term *kpr* is seldom used in secular contexts and is usually rendered 'atone.'"[23] Jacob appears to be getting closer to a posture of repentance. All of these gestures are gestures Jacob uses to control the situation. He is trying to be in control.

THE JOURNEY INVOLVES PRAYER

Jacob's prayer (Genesis 32:9-12) is the only extended prayer in the book of Genesis. Jacob first reminds God that he is doing what God told him to do. Then he expresses his appreciation for a God who met him when he crossed the Jordan "with only my staff" and for God's "steadfast love and all the faithfulness that you have shown to your servant." He recognizes that he is "not worthy of the least" of all the love and faithfulness. Brueggemann notes, "The word 'least' (v. 10) is not an incidental adjective, as we might conclude from the customary translations. It is the governing *ver*, 'I am smaller.' The self-identification of Jacob thus alludes to the stance against primogeniture. It is a primary theme of biblical faith that God's lot is cast with the little ones (Matthew 10:42; 18:6-14).

Jacob then gets to the point of his prayer, heard in the word "deliver" (Genesis 32:11). Jacob knows his life and his family's life are in danger. He knows that he must face the person from whom he stole the blessing and manipulated the birthright. Finally, Jacob comes back to God's promises: "I will do you good." Jacob tells God that he expects him to fulfill his promise.

THE JOURNEY INVOLVES WRESTLING WITH GOD

God is intertwined with human relations and human conflict. To deal with his estranged brother, Jacob needed to deal with God. After all of his planning and his prayer, in the midst of the risk, the anxiety and the fear, Jacob goes to sleep alone. During the night, when he is not in control, he wrestles with another all night, and the other, when he saw he was not going to prevail, put Jacob's hip out of joint. Jacob requests a blessing before he would stop the wrestling, as well as the name of the one with whom he is engaged. He does not get the name, but he gets a blessing with a name change, a new identity as Israel, as the other tells him, "For you have striven with God and with humans, and have prevailed" (Genesis 32:28). Brueggemann notes, "He has been named Jacob — 'heel/trickster/over-reacher/supplanter.' Each of these is true, but not flattering. Now he is 'Israel.' The etymology of 'Israel' is disputed. Perhaps it means 'God rules,' 'God preserves,' 'God protects.' But whatever the etymology, a new being has been called forth."[24] Jacob realizes that he has been wrestling with God: "For I have seen God face to face, and yet my life is preserved." Penuel means face of God.

The reason this text has experienced such rich and varied interpretations is that it is clothed in mystery and ambiguity. Jacob ultimately believes that he is wrestling with God, and his antagonist agrees. The antagonist also says that he has striven with humans. No doubt he is wrestling with Esau as well. Moreover, all of this for Jacob is a wrestling with himself, as he experiences a "new creation," a new identity. He is now Israel. The journey to reconciliation often involves a struggle with the human other, with God and with one's self. An encounter with the other can be transformative, as we stress in Chapter 5. One often emerges from such a journey a changed person.

JACOB LEARNS THE IMPORTANCE OF HUMILITY, VULNERABILITY AND RESTITUTION

The struggle ends for Jacob with a new identity and a limp; he is a more humble and vulnerable person. Jacob has learned some lessons from this struggle that give him a new spirit for engaging Esau. Earlier he had addressed Esau as his Lord. He approaches the meeting with Esau with extreme deference and humility: "He himself went on ahead of them, bowing himself to the ground seven times, until he came near his brother" (Genesis 33:3). His family bows down to Esau. He then repeats three times that he is seeking to "find favor in your eyes" (Genesis 33:8, 10, 15). A spirit of humility is essential in approaching the other whom you have wronged.

He approaches the meeting now with a limp. He brings a more vulnerable spirit to the engagement. This vulnerability along with the humility is a critical component in opening one's self and the other to the possibility of reconciliation.

Finally, Jacob recognizes the importance of restitution to restore Esau to some measure of what he stole from him. He brings great gifts. Esau says he does not need them, but then he accepts them. Wrongdoers need to make things right, and restitution is part of doing so.

These are essential aspects of restorative justice — responding to the harm created with real accountability, trying to make things right. We address this in greater detail when we study Matthew 18 in Chapter 3, and Abigail and Zaccheus in Chapter 7.

ESAU AND THE GIFT OF FORGIVENESS

We are learning much about how the offender Jacob is preparing for the engagement with the person he offended. We don't know what has been happening to Esau. The last we saw of him 20 years ago he had sworn to kill Jacob. Then all of a sudden he came out of the mist of time and "ran to meet him, and embraced him and fell on his neck and kissed him, and they wept" (Genesis 33:4). Esau did not arrive cautiously, but ran to meet Jacob. He did not wait for an apology, but embraced him, kissed him and wept. Both of them wept. This seems like a miracle. What enabled Esau to turn from the spirit of killing to the running, embracing spirit of forgiveness? Rebecca had hoped for a forgetting, telling her favorite son to "flee at once to my brother Laban in Haran, and stay with him for a while, until your brother's fury turns away — until your brother's anger against you turns away, and he forgets what you have done to him" (Genesis 27:43-45). Did Esau forget? What brought Esau to forgive and embrace Jacob? We will explore the journey of persons harmed in Chapters 4 to 6, concluding with a study of the Prodigal. Esau stands in the tradition of the welcoming parent of the Prodigal (Chapter 6). In Chapter 3 we see that his actions appear consistent with forgiving seventy times seven as described by Jesus in Matthew.

At the end of this meeting, Jacob and Esau part ways, never to meet again until the burial of their father Isaac (Genesis 35:29). The brothers go on to live their individual lives, with their different lifestyles. Does this show a respect for their unique and different personalities and needs, even as they are reconciled? Does this have to do with God's promise that Jacob will return to the promised land of Canaan, which is where Genesis Chapter 33 ends?

SEEING THE FACE OF GOD IN THE FACE OF ESAU

Jacob says to Esau after their embrace, "For truly to see your face is like seeing the face of God — since you have received me with such favor" (Genesis 33:10). This statement follows from two statements: (a) the statement of hope by Jacob as he journeys toward Esau that, after he atones with his gifts, even though unworthy, "I shall see his face" (Genesis 32:20), and

(b) the statement by Jacob after the wrestling, "For I have seen God face to face, and yet my life is preserved" (Genesis 32:30). The face motif concludes with Jacob seeing the face of God in Esau's face. In this moment of reconciliation, we cannot separate the divine and the human. The divine and the human are interconnected, and both are experienced whenever there is reconciliation, as we explore in Chapter 2. Jacob does see the face of God in the face of Esau.

The Use and Misuse of the Story

In the resource guide for the public television series "Talking About Genesis," Noam Zion, who is on the faculty of the Shalom Hartman Institute of Jerusalem, talks about the misuse of the Jacob story: "Just as Jacob successfully diverts the blessing for his benefit, many 'descendants of Jacob' have used the story to justify their triumphalism over contemporary rivals. In ancient Israel, it was the biological children of Jacob who claimed priority of blessing and of land over Abraham's less favored posterity — Ishmael, father of the Arabs; Lot, father of Moab and Amon (hence today's Amman, capital of Jordan); and especially Esau, father of the Edomites and the Amalekites. The Jews read a thousand years of acrimonious relations with their Semitic neighbor, Edom, into the sibling rivalry of Jacob and Esau."[25] Zion then goes on to point out how Christians used the story to show "God's inscrutable grace in the choice of the younger son, Jacob, who represented the Church, over the elder Esau, the Synagogue."[26]

How does a story of reconciliation become a story of division? We need to understand how we misuse the biblical story for psychological and political reasons. Zion concludes by saying,

> Millennia after the struggles of Jacob and Esau, each of us still claims to be the most beloved of God; we are each still in pursuit of the same patrimony of land, legitimacy, supremacy and blessing. In the stories of siblings, Genesis offers to ancient and modern Israel a model for understanding its ongoing life-and-

death struggles; the family feud offers a hopeful yet realistic image for these conflicts. Arabs and Jews are brothers sharing the same ancestors and the same humanity — we are all in the image of God. However, these brothers are not engaged merely in turf battles to be solved by pragmatic, diplomatic compromises and cleverly redrawn borders, but in issues of identity and dignity. We must work and pray for reconciliation or, at least, coexistence; my brother should not be demonized, but neither may I discount the possibility of fratricide. Idealism and realism must go hand in hand.[27]

In Chapter 8, we will turn to the theme of an Abrahamic family reunion.

Exercise

We have each had journeys that involve estrangement and attempts to overcome the estrangement. As authors, we know that we each have relationships that have not reconciled and some that have. Here you will have the opportunity to reflect on one of your own journeys by drawing a map of your journey. You are going to draw your own journey using symbols and words. Each of you will get a sheet of newsprint and several markers or pencils or crayons with which you will draw your map. You will have 10 to 15 minutes to draw your map. The map is primarily for personal reflection. This is not an artistic contest. As you draw your map, reflect on the following questions:

- What were the obstructions you had to overcome on the journey?
- What were some of the things that you did or happened to you that helped you reach a better place on the journey?
- Where are you now? Compare your map with that of Jacob's.
- What might you have taught Jacob?
- What might he teach you?
- Draw these lessons for the future as you continue to map the journey you have been on and the journey you are planning.

Then join a group of three or four. Here you will have an opportunity to describe what you want to describe about your map. You will not be pressed to discuss anything you do not want to discuss. Spend about 15 minutes in the small group. Remember that what is said is confidential. Then reconvene with the large group for the closing.

Concluding Ritual

The leaders invite each person to bring an object to the next study (Chapter 2) that symbolizes "love of God and neighbor" as experienced in their lives.

Silent Coptic Passing of the Peace: Everyone will stand. The leader will demonstrate the Coptic passing of the peace. This is done in silence. The leader turns to the person on her left. The leader touches her hands to her lips, and then holds her hands like a cup in front as the person to her left puts his hands underneath her hands and then circles her hands with his hands, scooping up the peace that is being passed. He then turns to the person on his left, touches his hands to his lips, then holds them like a cup in front as the person to his left puts her hands underneath his hands then circles his hands with her hands, scooping up the peace that is being passed. This is repeated around the Circle until it returns to the leader who scoops up the peace and ends with these words, "Go in peace."

Notes

20. Walter Brueggemann, *Genesis: Interpretation: A Bible Commentary for Teaching and Preaching* (Atlanta: John Knox Press, 1982), p. 229.

21. Susan Fiditch, "Genesis," in *The Women's Bible Commentary*, eds. Carol Newsom and Sharon H. Ringe (Louisville: Westminster John Knox Press, 1992), p. 16.

22. See, for example, the discussion of loving God, self and neighbor in Chapter 2. Dorotheos of Gaza says that we cannot experience either God or our fellow human beings without moving closer to each at the same time (p. 46).

23. Brueggeman, op. cit. p. 264.

24. Ibid, p. 268.

25. Noam Zion, in *Talking About Genesis, A Resource Guide* (New York: Doubleday, 1996), pp. 121-122.

26. Ibid, p. 122.

27. Ibid, p. 123.

Chapter 2

the relational nature of reality

the great commandment, the good news of reconciliation and the call to the ministry of reconciliation

"'You shall love the Lord your God with all your heart, and with all your soul, and with all your mind.' This is the greatest and first commandment. In addition, a second is like it: 'You shall love your neighbor as yourself.' On these two commandments hang all the law and the prophets."
—Matthew 22:37-39

So if anyone is in Christ, there is a new creation: everything old has passed away; see, everything has become new! All this is from God, who reconciled us to himself through Christ, and has given us the ministry of reconciliation.
—2 Corinthians 5:17-18a

Preparation

The Great Commandment: Love God, Neighbor and Self

- Read Matthew 22:34-40.
- In your journal write all of the questions you have about this text as well as your own reflections.
- Spend some time with your questions, letting these questions go deeper and deeper. Note your insights.
- Look at the questions we have asked and write down your thoughts as to where these questions lead you, which may include other questions.
- Spend some time with the text and your journaling before you turn to the reflections that follow that are focused on the Great Commandment.
- After you have read the Reflection sections, write down in your journal other insights and questions you have.

The Experience of Reconciliation and the Call to be Reconcilers

- Read 2 Corinthians 5:16-20.
- Again write down your questions and your reflections.
- Spend some time with your questions. Note your insights.
- Look at the questions we have asked and write down your thoughts as to where these questions lead you, which includes other questions.
- Spend some time with the text and your journaling before you turn to the Reflections.
- After you have read the Reflection, write down in your journal other insights and questions you have.
- Bring with you to the study an object that symbolizes for you the experience of the love of God and neighbor. For some, this might include, for example, the cross, a picture or drawing of a communion table covered with food to share with others, an engagement ring, a piece of bread. You will have the opportunity to tell the story of this object and what it symbolizes to you.

Setup

A small round table is in the middle of the room with a circle of chairs around the table. On the table is a single candle as well as a ball of yarn. Some light refreshments are in the room. Consider using a ball of yarn as a talking piece, a symbol of our relatedness, our being woven together in the fabric of God's creation.

Centering

The leader welcomes everyone as the candle is lighted.

Responsive Reading

> **Group Response:**
> **Teach us, O God, to know and radiate Your Love — within ourselves, for our neighbor and amid Your creation.**

The leader or a volunteer reads:

> Our deepest fear is not that we are inadequate; our deepest fear is that we are powerful beyond measure. It is our light, not our darkness that most frightens us. We ask ourselves, Who am I to be brilliant, gorgeous, talented, fabulous? Actually, who are you *not* to be? You are a child of God. Your playing small does not serve the world. There is nothing enlightened about shrinking so that other people won't feel insecure around you. We are all meant to shine, as children do. We were born to make manifest the glory of God that is within us. It's not just in some of us; it's in everyone. And as we let our own light shine, we unconsciously give other people permission to do the same. As we are liberated from our own fear, our presence automatically liberates others.[28]

Group Response: Teach us, O God, to know and radiate Your Love — within ourselves, for our neighbor and amid Your creation.

A volunteer reads the Story of the Good Samaritan (Luke 10:25-37):

Just then a lawyer stood up to test Jesus. "Teacher," he said, "what must I do to inherit eternal life?" He said to him, "What is written in the law? What do you read there?" He answered, "You shall love the Lord your God with all your heart, and with all your soul, and with all your strength, and with all your mind, and your neighbor as yourself." And he said to him, "You have given the right answer; do this, and you will live." But wanting to justify himself, he asked Jesus, "And who is my neighbor?" Jesus replied, "A man was going down from Jerusalem to Jericho, and fell into the hands of robbers, who stripped him, beat him, and went away, leaving him half dead. Now by chance a priest was going down that road, and when he saw him, he passed by on the other side. So likewise a Levite, when he came to the place and saw him, passed by on the other side. But a Samaritan while traveling came near him, and when he saw him, he was moved with pity. He went to him and bandaged his wounds, having poured oil and wine on them. Then he put him on his own animal, brought him to an inn, and took care of him. The next day he took out two denarii, gave them to the innkeeper, and said, 'Take care of him, and when I come back, I will repay you whatever more you spend.' Which of these three, do you think, was a neighbor to the man who fell into the hands of the robbers?" He said, "The one who showed him mercy." Jesus said to him, "Go and do likewise."

Group Response: Teach us, O God, to know and radiate Your Love — within ourselves, for our neighbor and amid Your creation.

Hymn
"God of the Sparrow, God of the Whale" (UMH #122)

Sharing of Stories
The ball of yarn is described and consensus is tested on using it as the talking piece.

    The ball of yarn is passed from left to right around the Circle as all are given the opportunity to tell the story of the object that they brought with them that represents something that relates to their experience of the love of God and neighbor. As each object is described, it is placed on the table.

Relational Covenant
The leader reminds everyone of the relational covenant that is posted on the wall. The covenant is read, and everyone affirms his or her commitment to the covenant.

Reading of the First Text
A volunteer will read Matthew 22:34-40.

Questions
Leader: What follows are just some suggested questions to help you formulate questions for group discussion. We would suggest having two or three questions prepared. Others will flow from the conversation. After each question you ask, use the talking piece passed around the Circle to the left, to hear all of the voices as participants respond to the question. Then hold the talking piece so that the conversation can flow naturally, building on what has been said. When you get to the second question, follow the same practice with the talking piece.

This session, unlike the previous session, has two sets of questions and two exercises. The first focuses on Matthew 22:34-40 and the second focuses on 2 Corinthians 5:17-18. Be sure to pace the questions and the exercises so that both passages can be explored.

- How do we love God?
- Who is neighbor to you?
- Jesus linked love of God and love of neighbor. Are they linked together in your experience? How?
- What impact does the Great Commandment have on you and your understanding of the world?
- Some of us were formed with a worldview that identifies strongly with individualism. What does the great commandment say to a worldview based on the autonomous individual?

REFLECTION | THE RELATIONAL NATURE OF REALITY

The reflections in this study are to stimulate your own thinking, finding what is meaningful to you in the passage. They are not intended to limit possible interpretations of the text.

The Great Commandment and the Relational Nature of Reality

In Matthew, two different texts from the Hebrew Bible, Deuteronomy 6:5, dealing with the love of God, and Leviticus 19:18, addressing love of neighbor, are combined.[29] This combination of the command to love God and love neighbor is distinctive in the teaching of Jesus. Here Jesus teaches us that to love God is related to loving your neighbor and loving the neighbor is related to loving God.

Dorotheos of Gaza, a sixth-century teacher, visualizes for us the connections between loving God and loving neighbor. One day the monks of his monastery came to him saying, "We have had it. We can't worship God in the company of our fellow monks." They used this wonderful phrase to describe their problem. It was one another's "ordinary, irritating presence" that got in the way. Does this sound familiar? We can understand how the monks felt.

Dorotheos responded by asking them to visualize the world as a great circle whose center is God and on whose circumference lies human lives. "Imagine now," he asked them, "that there are straight lines connecting from the outside of the circle all human lives to God at the center. Can't you see that there is no way to move toward God without drawing closer to other people, and no way to approach other people without coming near to God?"[30]

This story inspired the symbol for JustPeace.

Dorotheos understood that in order to get close to God we need to get closer and closer to our fellow human beings, and in order to get close to our fellow human beings we need to get closer to God. This is interesting, isn't it? God is intertwined with human relationships and human relationships are all intertwined with God. We experience the divine in, for example, our relationships, our marriages, in our working environments as we engage one another more deeply. Dorotheos says that we cannot experience either God or our fellow human beings without moving closer to each at the same time.

Roberta Bondi, who told this story in her book *Memories of God*, added,

There is something implied in the very shape of his imagined chart, however, that Dorotheos did not draw to the attention of his listeners — that in the movement toward love, whether of God, or of another human being, there is an open space so close to the center of reality, that human and the divine love become indistinguishable.[31]

Isn't this where we experience the incarnation?

Another perspective we would add relates to the fact that each of these human beings connected to the center is unique. Looking at God's creation, we know God loves differences. No two human beings have ever been identical. This means each relationship is unique. We need to respect the different relationships we have with one another and with God.

Another way to look at this circle is to suggest the circle is God and the center is the heart of God. In God, whether we recognize it or not, we all move and breathe and have our being (Acts 17:28). We live in God, who is closer than our breath. God is not only above or beyond but also among, within and between. God is the connective tissue of life. This vision is deeply incarnational. We are each a part of God's body. At the center, all creation comes together. The heart of God is where all is reconciled and made new. This is where we find our full humanity and our authentic selves. We experience our humanity and the divinity most fully when we experience a moment of reconciliation.

The vision of Dorotheos expresses the Great Commandment, to which we now turn, seeing how it is focused on love and relationships, describing a relational worldview.

LOVE GOD, NEIGHBOR AND SELF: THE SUM OF THE LAW AND THE PROPHETS

These commandments are a summary of both the law and the prophets. These two commandments are the Rosetta stone, the key hermeneutical lens through which all the law and prophets, the whole of the scripture and life, are to be understood and judged. Are this belief and this action informed by love of God, neighbor and self? If we understand and live this commandment, we will understand the heart and depth of all scriptures. Everything else is a footnote to this commandment.

We would add the insight Mark brings to the great commandment. Mark begins with the Shema, "Hear, O Israel: The Lord our God, the Lord is one" and ends with the statement that loving God and neighbor is more important "than all whole burnt offerings and sacrifices." We know how important these offerings and sacrifices were to the Jewish tradition of that time, but these simple acts of love are more important. We are also reminded of Amos 5:21-24: "I hate, I despise your feast, and I take no delight in your solemn assemblies. Even though you offer me your burnt offerings and cereal offerings, I will not accept them, and the peace offerings of your fatted beasts I will not look upon. Take away from me the noise of your songs; to the melody of your harps I will not listen. But let justice roll down like water, and righteousness like an ever-flowing stream." Mark then concludes by saying, "There is no other commandment greater than these." Loving God and neighbor is seen as one commandment.

LOVE GOD, NEIGHBOR AND SELF: THE GREAT COMMANDMENT

This is a commandment. This is not optional. We fail to do this at our peril and the peril of the world. This is the way the world is made. All boundaries are trumped by this commandment to love God, neighbor and self. When I dehumanize you, I dehumanize myself. When the toe is hurting, the whole body hurts. This is why broken relationships are so painful.

What does this tell us about the human condition, what we call sin? Sin is acting as if you are not interdependent and not in relation — acting as if God does not exist — being self-absorbed, self-occupied, not focusing on the relationship, the other and the self in relationship. Sin is the rupture of communion with God and our neighbor as well as with our own true self. In this anxious world, we are all guilty of this. Violence is the key manifestation of sin or evil, the destruction of communion. The judgment of the cross is the judgment of love — the judgment that fully exposes our shadow side.

Seen in the light of this reality, the way God created the world and created us for life together, we begin to see how critical and important forgiveness and reconciliation are to overcoming our broken relationships, in creating right relations.

LOVE GOD, NEIGHBOR AND SELF: IT'S ABOUT LOVE!

The action verb in this commandment is love. How do we understand God in the context of love? How do we love God? How do we love our neighbor? How do we love ourselves?

- **God is love.**

"Beloved, let us love one another, because love is from God, everyone who loves is born of God and knows God. Whoever does not love does not know God, for God is love" (1 John 4:7-8). Love is essential both to understanding the nature of God and the life we are called to live. We do experience the divine in simple acts of love. "No one has ever seen God; if we love one another, God lives in us, and [God's] love is perfected in us" (1 John 4:12).

Love defines God's very being. Love is the energy that connects us. God's love is incarnate in creation. God's love is not a limited commodity. God's love is abundant. Nothing can separate us from the love of God (Romans 8:38-39). In the darkest moments, we can say "Abba." We are able to love because God loves us (1 John 4:19).

- **To love God, we must love our neighbor.**

Love of neighbor is the most important way we express our love to God — as we recognize the image of God in each human being. If we love one another, God lives in us. To love is to know God. Love is the primary virtue. "If I speak in the tongues of mortals and of angels but do not have love, I am a noisy gong and a clanging cymbal" (1 Corinthians 13:1). In Matthew the great commandment is preceded by Jesus' teaching about the centrality of love and that "love of neighbor" includes the enemy (5:21-28 and 23-48). Luke moves to illustrate the commandment with the story of the Good Samaritan that addresses the question of who is my neighbor. In this story we find that the neighbor is anyone in need, such as the man who was robbed and beaten, but, even more important, that the neighbor is not just one of our clan or our religious community, the priest and the Levite, but the stranger, the Samaritan, the one who shows compassion. Our neighbor includes our enemies, and anyone in need.

- **We are to love our neighbor as we love ourselves.**

This verse assumes that we love ourselves as God loves us. Sometimes loving ourselves is the hardest of all. In the Great Commandment, loving ourselves is seen and experienced as we love our neighbor and love our God. This commandment contemplates a love of all three at the same time. To find oneself, the focus must shift from oneself to the neighbor and to God. As we focus on loving, loving God and neighbor, the self in relation comes into focus: the loving self, the compassionate self, the authentic self. This can be understood as losing oneself to find oneself (Luke 17:33). In short, we need to focus on loving and being led by love with all of our heart, soul, mind and strength.

LOVING GOD, NEIGHBOR AND SELF: IT'S ALL ABOUT RELATIONSHIPS!
If this scripture is the foundational text of the Bible, what does it tell us about the world God created in which we live? We would suggest that this scripture says: Creation is relational; God is a relational being; all of creation is related in God; we are who we are because of our relations.

- **Creation is relational.**

We are created for relationships with God and neighbors. John Paul Lederach notes, "At the cutting edge of fields from nuclear physics and biology to systems theory and organizational development, relationships are seen as the central organizing concept of theory and practice."[32] Lynn Margulis and Dorian Sagan theorize that new forms of life come into being through a symbiotic process and that cooperation and mutual dependence among all life forms are the central aspects of evolution. "The view of evolution as chronic bloody competition among individuals and species, a popular distortion of Darwin's notion of 'survival of the fittest,' dissolves before a new view of continual cooperation, strong interaction, and mutual dependence among life forms. Life did not take over the globe by combat, but by networking."[33] All creation evolves toward continued cooperation and mutual dependence. From quantum theory we learn, "Particles come into being and are observed only in relationship to something else. They do not exist as independent 'things.' . . . These unseen connections between what were previously thought to be separate entities are the fundamental elements of all creation."[34] Our own body is an example of this community of connections. Our bodies contain one quadrillion cells. Each human cell is made up of 400 billion molecules. At any one moment there is within our body one septillion cellular activities.

- **God is a relational being.**

As Martin Buber says, "In the beginning was the Relation."[35] The Trinitarian understanding of God describes God as a relational being. Early church leaders, and specifically John of Damascus, developed the theological term *perichoresis* to describe the mysterious relationship between the Father, Son and Holy Spirit. The term is made up of two Latin words, *peri* (circle or round, as in perimeter) and *choresis* (dancing, the root word used in choreography). In his book *Flame of Love*, Clark Pinnock writes of *perichoresis*: "The metaphor suggests moving around, making room, relating to one another without losing identity. The divine unity lies in the relationality of Persons, and the relationality is the nature of the unity. At the heart of this ontology is the mutuality and reciprocity among the Persons. Trinity means that shared life is basic to the nature of God. God is perfect sociality, mutuality, reciprocity and peace. As a circle of loving relationships, God is dynamically alive. There is only one God, but this one God is not solitary but a loving communion that is distinguished by overflowing life."[36]

- **All of creation is related in God.**

Through God we are all interconnected and interdependent. God is intertwined with all of our relations. As we noted earlier, in God, whether we recognize it or not, we all move and breathe and have our being. We are each a part of God's body. All is interconnected and interdependent in God.

This connection includes the whole of the cosmos — the whole of the created order — which we are to love and care for. One way we know God is through nature: "Ever since the creation of the world God's eternal power and divine nature, invisible though they are, have been understood and seen through the things he has made" (Romans 1:20). "The heavens are telling the glory of God, and the firmament proclaims his handiwork" (Psalm 19). The whole world is penetrated with the presence of God.

- **We are who we are because of our relations.**

The self is realized only in relation. Bishop Desmond Tutu has helped the world community understand the relational nature of creation. He says, "My humanity is caught up, is inextricably bound up, in yours. . . . A person is a person through other persons. . . . I am human because I belong. I participate. I share."[37] His understanding is informed by the African concept of *ubuntu* and the Christian concept of the Body of Christ. At the heart of *ubuntu* is an understanding that I am "diminished when others are humiliated or diminished, when others are tortured or oppressed, or treated as if they were less than who they are."[38] Paul says in the first letter to the Corinthians, "If one member suffers, all suffer together with it; if one member is honored, all rejoice together with it" (1 Corinthians 12:26). If we could only appreciate how we are dehumanized when we dehumanize another, we might consider our ways and actions differently.

Since we are all unique, all our relationships are unique, including our relationship with God. We need to respect the different relationships we have with one another and with God. Since we are created in the image of

God, we are called to focus on the relational nature of life, "to notice the connections." The relationship is greater than the sum of its parts. The vision is the "Beloved Community." The relationships are created and sustained by love.

In Mark's presentation of the Great Commandment, he demonstrates the possibility of reconciliation. In Mark, Jesus is in dialogue with a scribe. Unlike Matthew and Luke, where the Great Commandment is presented in the context of a challenge to Jesus by the Pharisees and by a lawyer, Mark has moved from confrontation to the unusual experience of an engagement with a sympathetic scribe. Here Jesus and the scribe bridge the gap witnessed in Matthew and Luke, finding a common faith — a moment of reconciliation.

Exercise

- As persons are able to do so, form a large circle with everyone standing separated and distant from one another. Imagine the round table at the center of the circle representing God.
- Move slowly toward the center (the worship table).
- When you get to the center stop, and in silence reflect on your feelings for a couple of minutes on this journey to the center and the experience at the center.
- Then share your thoughts out loud, one at a time, while standing at the center.
- Then imagine that God is the whole circle and the center is the heart of God.
- Reflect on this center as the heart of God. At the center, close to one another, do we find our full humanity and our authentic selves? Do we experience our humanity and the divinity most fully when we experience a moment of reconciliation?
- Now turn around and reflect on the journey back to the edge where you started as walking within the being of God.
- As you reflect on this exercise, how does it help you understand and experience the Great Commandment?
- Share your thoughts one at a time.

Reading of the Second Text
A volunteer will read 2 Corinthians 5:16-20.

Questions
Leader: What follows are just some suggested questions to help you formulate questions for group discussion. We would suggest having two or three questions prepared. Others will flow from the conversation. After each question you ask, use the talking piece passed around the Circle to the left, to hear all of the voices as participants respond to the question. Then hold the talking piece so that the conversation can flow naturally, building on what has been said. When you get to the second question, follow the same practice with the talking piece.

- Have you felt a need to be reconciled with God? What was this like?
- Have you experienced being reconciled with God? How?
- What is the ministry of reconciliation that has been given to us?

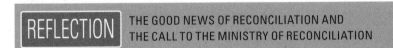

REFLECTION | THE GOOD NEWS OF RECONCILIATION AND THE CALL TO THE MINISTRY OF RECONCILIATION

These reflections are to stimulate your own thinking, not to limit the possible interpretations and the finding of what is meaningful to you in the passage.

The Experience of Reconciliation and the Call to be Reconcilers
How do we experience the spirit and the power to love God, to love our neighbor and love ourselves? How do we restore our broken relationships with God, neighbor and self?

CONTEXT
This scripture is the earliest discussion of the vocation of reconciliation in the Bible. It was written in the mid-50s CE.

Corinth was a leading Greek city that had been destroyed by the Romans in 146 BCE, then rebuilt 100 years later as a Roman colony. Corinth was prosperous as it was astride two major marine trade routes. There were large disparities between its new rich and its large laboring and slave classes. Corinth was a town that had a reputation as a place of wild living — drinking, promiscuity and unruly behavior. Peterson notes, "They were used to religions that offered wild rites for attaining enlightenment and immortality but didn't expect them to cultivate humility or give their hard-earned cash to the poor. They liked teachers with feel-good messages and religions that served the consumer. Paul was a shock."[39]

PAUL AND THE CHURCH IN CORINTH

Paul nurtured alternative communities he called *ekklesiai*. These churches, as envisaged by Paul, recognized "neither Jew nor Greek, neither slave nor free, neither male nor female" (Galatians 3:28). These churches were a new creation in which everything old has passed away and everything has become new. Paul refused to exclude Romans from these *ekklesiai*.

Paul was the founding pastor of the church in Corinth. This church gave him more problems than all of his other churches combined. He would address one problem and then more would appear. As Peterson says in his introduction to 2 Corinthians, "For anyone operating under the naive presumption that joining a Christian church is a good way to meet all the best people and cultivate smooth social relations, a reading of Paul's Corinthian correspondence is the prescribed cure. But however much trouble the Corinthians were to each other and to Paul, they prove to be a cornucopia of blessings to us, for they triggered some of Paul's most profound and vigorous writing."[40]

Paul spent a year and a half as the founding pastor of this church. After he left and started other churches, he received word that factions had developed and moral behavior had declined. There were problems with the way they ate together at the Lord's Supper, particularly how they mimicked the Roman class structure with the "higher class eating with the host in the dining room while lower-class participants ate in the porticoes and received leftover food (1 Corinthians 11:17-34)."[41]

There is a lost letter referred to in 1 Corinthians 5:9. Paul's second letter, 1 Corinthians, was very pastoral and gave them clear guidance — some of it hard for people to hear, such as those guilty of moral wrongdoing or participants in lawsuits, or those who ate food offered to idols. Paul made a second trip that was not successful and was painful to him. After this trip came a letter written in tears (2 Corinthians 2:4), a stern letter. Paul wanted them to feel his love and deep concern for them and at the same time to demand that they hold accountable the open rebel who was leading the opposition (2 Corinthians 2:6). This letter made a difference. 2 Corinthians is a thankful letter and a response to the attack on his leadership, on his authority. Paul had been challenged by the Jewish Christians to make the non-Jewish Christians adopt the practices and conventions of the Mosaic Law. Paul was trying to build a church for all people.

PAUL AND RECONCILIATION

Christopher Marshall says in his book *Beyond Retribution*, "Reconciliation is the central or unifying theme in Paul's theology."[42] In his work on peace in the New Testament, Willard Swartley shows how peace and reconciliation are the center of New Testament theology and ethics.[43] In regard to Paul's theology, Swartley says, "Rather, the notion of making peace between humans and God and between formerly alienated humans is so central to the core of Pauline doctrinal and ethical thought that it is impossible to develop a faithful construal of Pauline thought without peacemaking and/or reconciliation at the core."[44]

A NEW CREATION

"From now on, therefore, we regard no one from a human point of view; even though we once knew Christ from a human point of view, we know him no longer in that way. So if anyone is in Christ, there is a new creation: everything old has passed away; see, everything has become new! All this is from God" (2 Corinthians 5:16-18a).

No longer do we view life and reality from a human point of view, or, as stated in the Greek, according to the flesh. For Paul, the flesh, *sarkis*, was not our physical bodies or even our sexuality. *Sarkis*, as Ched Myers and Elaine Enns note, is "one of Paul's favorite metaphors for the deeply rooted, socially conditioned worldview we inherit from our upbringing. It is the sum total of personal and political constructs and conventions that define what it means to be a member of a given culture — in other words, the way most folk think and act."[45] They go on to say, "A key example of the perspective of the 'flesh' . . . is the dominant assumption that the 'moral' response to violation is punishment. To challenge this cultural conviction quickly engenders passionate and often irrational resistance that is both broad (i.e., the majority opinion) and deep (welling up from the core of individual psyches). This is the power of the 'flesh' in Paul's sense."[46] For Walter Wink, this worldview is the "domination system" that worships the "myth of redemptive violence," the belief that violence can save us.[47]

For Paul those who are in communion with Christ have adopted a radically new perspective (2 Corinthians 5:17). Now we look at life from the perspective of God as seen in the life, teachings, death and resurrection of Jesus the Christ. To be "in Christ" is to experience the incarnation — the divine in the human. To be "in Christ" is to imitate Jesus, being conformed to his image. For Swartley, this means living a life that does not lead "to rivalry and violence, but to building others up, avoiding scandal, preferring one another, empowering the other and non-retaliation against evil in order that as members of the community of the new creation we break the spiral of violence and become the strands of yarn that by God's Spirit are knitted into the display of love, justice, and shalom."[48]

God Reconciles: Reconciliation as God's Initiative

"All this is from God, who reconciled us to himself through Christ, and has given us the ministry of reconciliation: that is, in Christ God was reconciling the world to himself, not counting their trespasses against them, and entrusting the message of reconciliation to us" (2 Corinthians 5:18-19).

God reconciles. The work of reconciliation comes from God's initiative.

The power of reconciliation comes from God. The human world in its self-centeredness is separated from God. In our human relations we are torn apart by violence, hatred, retribution and apathy. How do we restore the relationship with God and with our neighbors? We cannot, alone! Only the Love that created and connects us has the ultimate power to reconnect us. On the cross we see it all come together — the violence, the response to Jesus by the principalities and the powers, and the experience in the midst of the violence of feeling abandoned by God and neighbor. Here we recognize this is not just the experience of a human being but of God as well, who shares our experience. Here we see that human violence not only affects God's relational world but is an attack on God's relational being. The Good News is God and the relation cannot be destroyed. Love is stronger than violence and death, and the way of God, which is the only way out of the cycles of violence and retribution, is the way of forgiveness and love.

In this relational world of difference, God's love is at work for right relations and a culture of *justpeace*. God's goal for all creation is *shalom* — well-being and right relations, with God, with neighbor and with one's self. This is experienced in the reconciling acts of God. In Jesus, we see that God is present in our world, suffers with all creation on the cross, and breaks the grip of the principalities and powers through the word of forgiveness on the cross. In the resurrection, we find victory over death and a new creation. Receiving this power-filled gift, we can do likewise, experiencing the spirit and the energy to reconcile with the neighbor as well as ourselves.

This reconciliation is not just for me, as an individual. It is for us. In fact, it is for the whole of the cosmos. Empowered by the reconciliation God offers us, we need to respond. God's reconciliation not only empowers us to do likewise but also mandates we participate in a "ministry of reconciliation."

We Are Called to Be Reconcilers

> All this is from God, who reconciled us to himself through
> Christ, and has given us the ministry of reconciliation: that is, in
> Christ God was reconciling the world to himself, not counting

> *their trespasses against them, and entrusting the message of*
> *reconciliation to us. So we are ambassadors for Christ, since God*
> *is making his appeal through us; we entreat you on behalf of*
> *Christ, be reconciled to God.*
>
> —2 Corinthians 5:18-20

To participate in this reconciliation we are called to embrace the "minis-try of reconciliation" (2 Corinthians 5:18). Reconciliation is our vocation. This vocation is "given" to us. We have received a great gift. However, it is more than gift. We are "ambassadors for Christ." Ambassadors represented the Roman Empire, especially in foreign lands. As Myers and Enns as-sert, "While Caesar's envoys throughout the Mediterranean world strove to defeat enemies and to bend nations and peoples to the will of the *Pax Romana*, the emissaries of Christ were to appeal to those same nations and peoples to be reconciled to God and one another (2 Corinthians 5:20b)."[49]

Reconciliation is an act of developing a new relationship that is just and right. God calls us to share the message of reconciliation and practice the ministry of reconciliation. This is a holistic ministry: evangelism and social justice or social holiness. Charles Villa-Vicencio, a theologian in South Africa, says, "That, in brief, is why I (a Christian minister, a theologian and a social scientist) have chosen to work on the staff of the Commission![50] It is because I believe that if the Christian faith does not ultimately contribute to healing and reconciliation — which involves the difficult process of con-fession, repentance, reparation and forgiveness (and there are no shortcuts!), the gospel is little more than celestial escapism."[51]

The role of the reconciler is to stand in the gaps, often tragic gaps, and help those estranged understand one another. As reconcilers, we see the gap between what is and what could or should be in the relationship, between reality and possibility. We live in the tension, helping persons and com-munities see a life-giving way. Living in the tension, we never succumb to seeing only what is, to becoming cynical, nor do we just see pure possibility separated from reality and become irrelevant idealists.

Reconciliation is not a hasty process, proclaiming peace where there is no peace, ignoring injustice and human suffering. Reconciliation is intimately connected with God and right relations. As Christians, we must restore the work of reconciliation from the periphery to the center of the life and witness of the Church where it belongs. Imagine if every church became a Neighborhood Reconciliation Center.

Exercise
- Divide into groups of two or three.
- Consider together how a United Methodist congregation can become a Neighborhood Reconciliation Center.
- What will it do?
- What will it mean for its own members?
- What will it do for the community?
- What will its worship look like?
- Record all of your ideas and decide how you will follow up with leaders in your congregation or together in a neighboring congregation.

Concluding Ritual
The leader asks the Circle members to bring objects to the next study session that symbolize forgiveness, restorative justice and or reconciliation in their life.

Conclude with a ritual around making a web with the ball of yarn. The leader will take the ball of yarn, holding on to the end of yarn and toss it to another member of the Circle. The recipient will hold the yarn tightly between herself or himself and the leader and then toss it to another member. Each member will do likewise. The last member to receive the yarn will toss it back to the leader, who will say, "Here we see how we are interconnected and interdependent. We are part of the web of relationships. May we 'become the strands of yarn that by God's Spirit are knitted into the display of love, justice and *shalom*,' into the new creation of reconciliation. Go in peace."

Notes

28. Marianne Williamson, *A Return to Love: Reflections on the Principles of a Course in Miracles* (New York: Harper Collins, 1992), pp. 190-191. Note: Sometimes attributed to the inaugural address of Nelson Mandela.

29. See also Mark 12:28-34 and Luke 10:25-28.

30. Roberta Bondi's paraphrase of "Dorotheos of Gaza: Discourses and Sayings," trans. Eric Wheeler (Minneapolis: Cistercian Publishers, 1977), pp. 138-139, in Roberta Bondi, *Memories of God: Theological Reflections on a Life* (Nashville: Abingdon Press, 1995), p. 201.

31. Bondi, op. cit., p. 201.

32. John Paul Lederach, *The Moral Imagination* (London: Oxford University Press, 2005), p. 34.

33. Lynn Margulis and Dorion Sagan, *Microcosmos: Four Billion Years of Evolution from Our Microbial Ancestors* (New York: HarperCollins, 1986), pp. 14-15.

34. Margaret J. Wheatley, *Leadership and the New Science*, 2nd edition (San Francisco: Berrett-Koehler Publishers, 1999), pp. 9, 11.

35. Martin Buber, *I and Thou,* trans. Walter Kaufmann (New York: Charles Scribner's Sons, 1970), p. 69.

36. Clark Pinnock, *Flame of Love* (Downers Grove, Ill.: InterVarsity Press, 1997), p. 31.

37. Desmond Mpilo Tutu, *No Future Without Forgiveness* (New York: Image, Doubleday, 1999), p. 31.

38. Ibid. p. 31.

39. Eugene Peterson, *The Message Remix, The Bible in Contemporary Language* (Colorado Springs: NAVPRESS, 2003), p. 1690.

40. Ibid. p. 1690.

41. Ched Myers and Elaine Enns, *Ambassadors of Reconciliation*, Vol. I (New York: Orbis Books, 2009), p. 8.

42. Christopher Marshall, *Beyond Retribution: A New Testament Vision for Justice, Crime and Punishment* (Grand Rapids: Wm. B. Eerdmans Publishing Co., 2001), p. 463. See also Ralph P. Martin, *Reconciliation: A Study of Paul's Theology* (London, U.K.: Marshall, Morgan & Scott), 1981.

43. Willard Swartley, *Covenant of Peace: The Missing Peace in New Testament Theology and Ethics* (Grand Rapids: Wm. B. Eerdmans Publishing Co., 2006), p. 191.

44. Ibid, p. 102. See also Col. 1:15-23, Rom. 5:1-11 and Eph. 2:11-22.

45. Myers and Enns, op. cit., p. 10.

46. Ibid.

47. Walter Wink, *The Powers That Be: Theology for a New Millennium* (New York: Doubleday, 1998), p. 42.

48. Swartley, op. cit., p. 375.

49. Myers and Enns, op. cit., p. 12.

50. We address The Truth and Reconciliation Commission in subsequent chapters. For a brief overview, see p. 173 in the Appendix.

51. Charles Villa-Vecencio, "On Taking Responsibility," in *To Remember and To Heal*, eds. Russel Botman and Robin M. Petersen (Cape Town, South Africa: Human and Rousseau, 1996), p. 132.

Chapter 3

the practice of forgiveness, restorative justice and reconciliation
the jesus way

"If another member of the church sins against you, go and point out the fault when the two of you are alone. If the member listens to you, you have regained that one. But if you are not listened to, take one or two others along with you, so that every word may be confirmed by the evidence of two or three witnesses. If the member refuses to listen to them, tell it to the church, and if the offender refuses to listen even to the church, let such a one be to you as a Gentile and a tax collector."

—Matthew 18:15-17

Preparation
- Read Matthew 18.
- In your journal write all of the questions you have about this text as well as your own reflections.
- Reflect on the way the pieces of the chapter work together.
- Spend some time with your questions, letting these questions go deeper and deeper. Note your insights.

- Look at the questions we have asked and write down your thoughts as to where these questions lead you, which may include other questions.
- Spend some time with the text and your journaling before you turn to the reflections that follow.
- After you have read the Reflection section, write down in your journal other insights and questions you have.
- Bring with you to the study, if you are comfortable doing so, an object that symbolizes for you an experience of forgiveness, restorative justice and or reconciliation in your life. For us, this might be a letter, a picture, a gift, an agreement, a Kleenex, a coin, for example.
- You will have the opportunity to tell the story of this object, if you are willing, and what it symbolizes to you.
- You can simply place your object on the table in the middle when you hold the talking piece if you are not comfortable telling the story at this time. You can simply pass if you do not bring an object.

Setup

A small round table is in the middle of the room with a circle of chairs around the table. On the table is a single candle as well as a Bible. Some light refreshments are in the room. Consider using the Bible as a talking piece, our guide to this practice of forgiveness, restorative justice and reconciliation.

Centering

The leader welcomes everyone as the candle is lighted.

Call to the Table

> *When you have a problem,*
>> **You come to the table.**
> *When you are hungry,*
>> **You come to the table.**
> *When you have a disagreement,*
>> **You come to the table.**

When you want to get some work done,
> **You come to the table.**

When you worship in the spirit of Christ,
> **You come to the table.**

Centering Prayer

O God Creator, God Redeemer, God Great Spirit in us all,
Be here among us at your table. Breathe through our burdened frame the spirit of your peace. Let your Wisdom flow within our conversation, let the bounty of your land fill up our empty hands, let the water of your well of mercy quench our thirsty faith. Renew us in this time together; send us out to heal your world. May it be so. Amen.

Prayer of Confession

We confess that the circle of love is repeatedly broken because of our sin of exclusion. We create separate circles: the inner circle and the outer circle, the circle of power and the circle of despair, the circle of privilege and the circle of deprivation.

Forgive us our sins as we forgive all who have sinned against us.

We confess that the circle of love is broken whenever there is alienation, whenever there is misunderstanding, whenever there is insensitivity or a hardening of the heart.

Forgive us our sins as we forgive all who have sinned against us.

We confess that the circle of love is broken whenever we cannot see eye to eye, whenever we cannot link hand in hand, whenever we cannot live heart to heart and affirm our differences.

Forgive us our sins as we forgive all who have sinned against us.

Through God's grace we are forgiven, by the mercy of our Creator, through the love of the Christ, and the power of the Spirit.

Let us rejoice and be glad! Glory to God! Amen.
— *Miriam Therese Winter, 1987*

The leader tests consensus on using the Bible as a talking piece. Using the talking piece, the leader invites those who brought an object that says something about her or his own experience of forgiveness, restorative justice and or reconciliation to put the object on the "altar," the table. If you are comfortable doing so, describe the object you brought with you and its meaning for you. If you are uncomfortable doing so, just place the object on the table when the talking piece comes to you.

Relational Covenant

The leader reminds everyone of the relational covenant that is posted on the wall. The covenant is read, and everyone affirms his or her commitment to the covenant.

Reading of the Text

Ask for a volunteer or volunteers to read Matthew 18.

Questions

Leader: What follows are just some suggested questions to help you formulate questions for group discussion. We would suggest having four or five questions prepared. Others will flow from the conversation. After each question you ask, use the talking piece passed around the Circle to the left to hear all of the voices as participants respond to the question. Then hold the talking piece so that the conversation can flow naturally, building on what has been said. When you get to the second question, follow the same practice with the talking piece.

- What does it mean to you when Jesus says, "Be like a child?" How does this relate to being a reconciler?
- How do you experience God's presence in the midst of conflict and harm?
- Does this chapter offer some guideposts for helping you respond to someone who harms you?
- Does this chapter offer some guideposts for helping you respond when you harm someone?
- What does it mean to forgive "seventy times seven?"
- How do you respond to the harsh reality of this chapter that deals with not forgiving and not listening?

 **REFLECTION** THE PRACTICE OF FORGIVENESS, RESTORATIVE JUSTICE AND RECONCILIATION

These reflections are to stimulate your own thinking, not to limit the possible interpretations and the finding of what is meaningful to you in the passage.

The Jesus Way

What does the journey of reconciliation look like? How do we practice this calling? In all of our readings on forgiveness, reconciliation, conflict transformation and restorative justice, we have found nothing more helpful than Matthew 18, a book of instruction to the early church. Here is where the scripture puts flesh and blood on the bones of the Great Commandment and on our Calling to be Ministers of Reconciliation as we described in Chapter 2.

The following schema should help you visualize the message of Matthew 18, which will be elaborated on in this chapter.

Matthew 18
The Church as a Place for the Engagement of Conflict and for Justice and Reconciliation

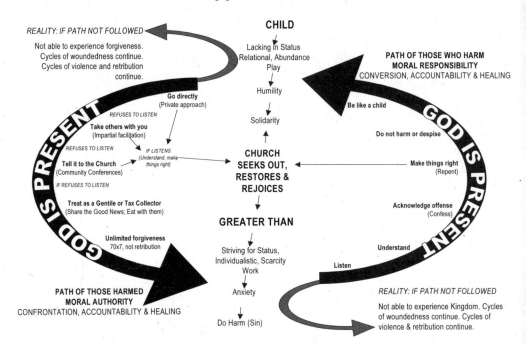

Matthew Chapter 18 begins and ends with two of the greatest sources of conflict and harm: power and money. The chapter begins with the question from the disciples of Jesus: "Who is the greatest in the kingdom of heaven?" It ends with the issue of the forgiveness of debt. One whose debt is bigger than all of the debt of Mesopotamia is forgiven. This debtor then turns on his small debtor, throws him into jail and subsequently suffers the consequences of one who is forgiven but does not forgive. In between, we are given

- an analysis as to why we have destructive conflict and violence — the problems created by trying to be greater than another;
- an understanding that God is present with us in the midst of conflict;
- an understanding of why Jesus calls us to be "like a child," or what it means to say peacemakers, reconcilers, are children of God;

- practical advice on how to deal with conflict and harm: the journey of reconciliation, the journey of restorative justice;
- the story of the lost sheep, with its vision of no one being lost and the celebration that occurs when restoration of relationship takes place;
- the radical breaking of cycles of woundedness, retribution and violence through the act of forgiveness; and
- an understanding of the deep reality of creation, seeing the consequence of not following the path of reconciliation and restorative justice, being told that if we do not forgive we will not be able to experience forgiveness and that if we do not follow the journey of responding to those we have harmed we will not be able to experience the Kingdom.

God is present with us in the midst of conflict.

In the middle of Matthew 18 is the verse "For where two or three are gathered in my name, I am there among them" (18:20). While we may often think of this as any church gathering, even a potluck, in this scripture we find ourselves in the midst of conflict and in the midst of the community confronting and healing offenses. The journey of reconciliation is a journey that no one takes alone. God heals, God restores and God saves. The only question we have is whether we really believe this. The more we work with conflict, the more we are aware that this is where we find God most fully present.

Seeking Out Those Who Are Lost, Restoring Them and Having a Great Celebration

The heart and soul of this chapter is the parable of the shepherd in search of the lost sheep. Everything in the chapter is seen in the context of this parable.

> What do you think? If a shepherd has a hundred sheep, and
> one of them has gone astray, does he not leave the ninety-nine
> on the mountains and go in search of the one that went astray?
> (Matthew 18:12-14)

Here we see the understanding of *ubuntu* or *shalom* elevated to a new level. In this relational world, God desires that no one is to be lost. This means no one, which includes both those who are lost because they have caused harm and those who have been harmed.

Today we seem to be worried about making sure we keep what we have or about not losing more than we have been losing, living out of a theology of scarcity. We want to make sure we keep the 99 and not lose any of them while we go off looking for the one who is missing. What if we experienced ourselves as the Beloved Community or Body of Christ, as Paul did, understanding that when the toe is hurting, the whole body hurts. In the body, we see how each of us is affected by the joy and pain of the other parts. Aren't we all served when the shepherd seeks out the one who is lost? What if we all were shepherds? What if the 99 all seek out the lost together? The health of the community is determined by how the least and the lost are treated. This is not just about individual but communal healing and reconciliation. What blesses one blesses all. All work together for the good of the whole.

The return of the one who is lost calls for rejoicing. What if every Sunday became a celebration over the return to community of someone who had been lost?

> Ubuntu speaks particularly about the fact that you can't exist as a human being in isolation. It speaks about our interconnectedness. You can't be human all by yourself, and when you have this quality — Ubuntu — you are known for your generosity.
>
> We think of ourselves far too frequently as just individuals, separated from one another, whereas you are connected and what you do affects the whole world. When you do well, it spreads out; it is for the whole of humanity.
>
> — Desmond Mpilo Tutu,
> *No Future Without Forgiveness*
> (New York: Image, Doubleday,1999)

THE BEING OF THE RECONCILER/PEACEMAKER: BEING LIKE A CHILD

How do we become a reconciler, a peacemaker? In the Beatitudes, Jesus associates being a child of God with being a peacemaker. Eugene Peterson helps us understand Jesus' vision in his paraphrase of Matthew 5:9: "You're blessed when you can show people how to cooperate instead of compete or fight. That's when you discover who you really are, and your place in God's family." [52] Being a peacemaker is discovering who you really are, discovering what it means to be fully human. For Jesus, this means to be converted to being like a child — a child of God.

In Matthew 18 in response to the question by the disciples, "Who is the greatest in the kingdom of heaven?" Jesus answers by putting a child "among them" (Matthew 18:1-2). Jesus says, "Truly I tell you, unless you change and become like children, you will never enter the kingdom of heaven. Whoever becomes humble like this child is the greatest in the kingdom of heaven"(Matthew 18:3-4). [53] The first thing that happens in this scripture is that Jesus turns our world upside down and puts those seeking to be the greatest at the bottom and the child, who was the least in Roman culture, at the top, defining the child as the greatest. What is Jesus trying to tell us through this social reversal? What problems are created by striving to be greater than another, whether it is in power, money, sex, goodness, or even humility? In a conflicted and violent world, why should human beings be like a child? Is it even possible?

We should recognize that Jesus' proposition sounds as strange today to us as it did to his disciples. We understand Nicodemus' question: "How can anyone be born after growing old" (John 3:4)? Wouldn't we all like to grow up, gain a little maturity, be a wise elder, and put away some childish things? Why would we want to be like a child? We know that being like a child as a mature person cannot be a return to naiveté or ignorance of the world. It is not about being childish, as we are also told to put away childish things (1 Corinthians 13:11). As "mature" people, however, Jesus tells us we must change. We need to be converted and the conversion is described as becoming like a child.

Not only do we have these reactions, but we are also aware that this image may be troubling to people who have not been treated as equals or as fully human with the respect they deserve. We are also aware that childhood is complex and we all have positive as well as negative experiences with children.

Recently we have begun to connect this calling with the vision of the peacemaker as the child of God. Struggling with the strangeness of this proposition, we have come to appreciate the reality, the maturity and the wisdom of the conversion to be "like a child" that Jesus seeks in all of us, including peace builders. We have come to believe we can learn what it means to be a peacemaker by understanding what it means to be like a child.

Let Go of Striving for Status or Control

In Roman society the child had the least status of anyone. The child was simply property. The child was the most vulnerable. Children had no rights. The first thing Jesus is telling us is that the life to which he calls us is not about striving for status. In fact, it is about being in solidarity with those with no status. For Jesus, the child is representative of the widow, the orphan, the alien. Jesus says, "Whoever welcomes one such child in my name welcomes me" (Matthew 18:5). To "receive a child," to be in solidarity with the least, is to receive Jesus himself.

Jesus' negative response to the question of who is the greatest in heaven is not, for us, a statement that we are not great or should not express our greatness. We are reminded of the statement in Chapter 2 from Mary Ann Williamson, author of *A Return to Love*.

> Our deepest fear is not that we are inadequate. Our deepest
> fear is that we are powerful beyond measure! It is our Light,
> not our darkness, that frightens us. We ask ourselves, who am
> I to be brilliant, gorgeous, talented and fabulous? Actually,
> who are you *not* to be? You are a child of God. Your playing
> small doesn't serve the world. There's nothing enlightened

about shrinking so that other people won't feel insecure around you. We are born to make manifest the Glory of God that is within us. It's not just in some of us. It's in everyone. And as we let our own Light shine, we unconsciously give other people permission to do the same. As we are liberated from our fears, our presence automatically liberates others.[54]

In short, as those created in the image of God, we are filled with greatness, with abundant gifts and resources.

The problem for Jesus is not our being great, but our striving to be greater than another, living out of scarcity, out of not enough power, love or resources. It is a life of comparison, anxious expectations, and the need to prove oneself instead of simply being authentically yourself, letting your song be sung, your calling lived fully. Trying to be greater than another leads not only to a lack of neighborliness but also to idolatry — worship of money and power, for example. For Jesus, trying to be greater is the problem of the "domination system." Described by Walter Wink, the domination system is a system "characterized by unjust economic relations, oppressive political relations, biased race relations, patriarchal gender relations, hierarchical power relations, and the use of violence to maintain them all."[55]

Being a child is also not about striving to control. Seeking status and seeking control go together in our anxious and fearful lives. One of the most important epiphanies I (Tom) have experienced happened on the flight to South Africa for my sabbatical in 1996. You probably do not know this, but lawyers can be very controlling. I had this vision of myself as a sailor in a sailboat with the sail closely hauled, going up against the wind, and with my hand firmly gripping the tiller, directing the boat in the direction I wanted it to go. I was in control. I then began to look at my life as a trial lawyer. I thought I controlled a courtroom; as a managing partner of a law firm I thought I had some control over a law firm. What happened next was the sensation of letting out the sail, going with the wind or the Spirit, and loosening my grip on the tiller to a very light touch. I can remember feeling my whole body relax and the rush that came with the feeling that I was going with the wind, with the Spirit. This letting go of striving to control was one of the most significant moments in my life. I still make lists and I still have a grip, although generally looser, on the tiller, but my primary goal and experience is letting go and going with the Spirit. And the Spirit has taken me, first in South Africa and ever since, to places much better and more interesting than any place I was striving to steer my boat. I have found myself and my own well-being when I have allowed the Spirit to lead me.

DEVELOP RELATIONSHIPS OF RESPECT AND TRUST

Matthew 18 contains one of the most intimate descriptions of being related to God. Jesus says, "Take care that you do not despise one of these little ones; for, I tell you, in heaven their angels continually see the face of my Father in heaven" (Matthew 18:10). Peterson paraphrases this to say that "their personal angels are constantly in touch with my Father in heaven."[56] This is one of the most extraordinary scriptures in the Bible. How intimate and close to God! Children live in the presence of God as they are born knowing they are dependent and related. There is a natural sense of being interconnected and interdependent. Children know that it is all about re-lationships and "simple trust." With Martin Buber, children know that "in the beginning is the Relation."[57]

Seeking to be greater than another is driven by an autonomous, indi-vidualistic view of reality — a denial of the relational nature of life and the reality that we find our true selves in community. The problem is not the greatness or importance of the individual but the ideology of individualism. This autonomous individualistic view of reality is deeply ingrained in our culture. Being like a child is particularly countercultural for us. We live as if we believe that we are self-made.

Peacemakers, children of God, are those who know that it is all about relationships, with God, neighbor and self.

Bring a Sense of Gratitude and Abundance to the Work of Peace Building

A child has not earned anything. A child, who is a gift to the world, receives life as a gift, and the gift is sufficient and abundant. Each child is sacred, gifted and great. The child sees life through eyes of wonder and awe. Hopefulness is typically natural and essential to a young child.

Power and love are not limited by God. The child is not born with a sense of scarcity, but soon the child begins to experience human-made scarcity, some, tragically, in a very short period of time. Seeking to be greater than another is driven by this fear of scarcity, a fear that there is never enough. A peace builder, a child of God, brings to situations of conflict and harm a sense of gratitude and abundance.

Express Humility as Awe and Wonder

Is play the fullest expression of gratitude to God, gratitude for the gift of abundant life, which we have not earned or created ourselves, gratitude for the actions of God reconciling us and the cosmos to God's self? The act of playing out of gratitude is, for us, the expression of humility experienced as wonder. This is being related to God, not believing we are gods. This comes from knowing that God is in control, not us, and that God's creation is worthy of awe and wonder. This seems to be what Jesus means when he asks us to become "humble like this child" (Matthew 18:4). This is not about humiliation or the acceptance of a subservient status. This is not about being inferior, or not feeling that you are of sacred worth. Recognizing that the God of wonder and awe is in control frees us from burdens that we do not need to carry — like the striving to be greater, trying to change anyone other than ourselves, and feeling that if we ourselves do not do it that it won't get done. Being humble is receiving life as a gift, not something that we have created.

Be in Solidarity with all Creation

The end result of being like a child is being in solidarity and community with God and neighbor, even with the "enemy." We were made for community. In Jesus' training manual for disciples, The Sermon on the Mount, he instructed his disciples, "Don't react violently against the one who is evil" (Matthew 5:39, Scholars Version). Instead, "Love your enemies and pray for those who persecute you" (Matthew 5:44). We are to be in community even with our enemies.

Does a sense of scarcity and striving for status and control destroy community by creating fear and anxiety? Reinhold Niebuhr says that "anxiety is the precondition to sin."[58] Doesn't this fear and anxiety lead to offenses and harm to others, particularly the "least?" Doesn't it create systems of domination and exploitation? Doesn't it create stumbling blocks, the literal meaning of the Greek word that is translated as sin? Are there consequences? Jesus tells us, "But if you give them [children] a hard time, bullying or taking advantage of their simple trust, you'll soon wish you hadn't. You'd be better off dropped in the middle of the lake with a millstone around your neck. Doom to the world for giving those God-believing children a hard time! Hard times are inevitable, but you don't have to make it worse — and it's doomsday to you if you do" (Peterson's paraphrase of Matthew 18:6-7).[59]

What Jesus has opened up for us by this juxtaposition of being a child to the question of who is the greatest in heaven is an analysis of why we have destructive conflict and harm in this world, the destruction of community. It comes from trying to be greater than another, dominating or exploiting others. It ultimately comes from not having the spirit of the child.

Peacemakers, children of God, are those who seek God's *shalom*: well-being and right relations for all creation. They see the humanity of the participants in any process and feel a connection with each person. They truly believe that human beings can come together and find connections with one another — common ground as well as higher ground. Recognizing their own privileged position in life, they experience the truth of Paul's statement that it is as you lose yourself in loving engagement with others that you find your true self. We do like Peterson's paraphrase of Matthew 5:9, "You're blessed when you can show people how to cooperate instead of compete or fight. That's when you discover who you really are, and your place in God's family." This is an extraordinary gift if we can help people who are in conflict discover who they really are and their place in God's family, with one another.

PRACTICAL PATH OF THOSE HARMED

After the parable of the lost sheep, Jesus describes the journey of being restored to community for both the person who is harmed and the one doing the harm, to the child who has been harmed and to the one seeking to be the greatest. As we go down the path of those harmed and the path of the one who harms, we recognize we have been on both paths ourselves, often simultaneously, experiencing harm and doing harm. In fact, it is our experience that in most cases it is important to recognize this, to name the fact that all parties have experienced harm. This recognition often frees the parties to move forward together. As a party to the conflict, admitting to the other party your role in the harm and your recognition that the other has been harmed is significant in opening up a healing process.

Jesus starts with the path of the person harmed, as does restorative justice, with victims and their harm. The person harmed has priority. Jesus has the victim (the one harmed) going to the offender (the one creating the harm). He is saying that victims have the moral agency or authority. He says that they should be empowered to confront and to hold accountable the one who has harmed them. The person harmed is the primary moral agent for transformation. The victim is not powerless. For Jesus, this is a way to healing. We address the confrontation of the other with the requisite truth-telling in Chapter 5.

As will be discussed, this confrontation is not about revenge but about restitution, amends, making things right. This path is not a path of punishment, but a path of accountability and restoration. This is a demanding process. What is the process for dealing with "sin" — with the harm created by another?

- *Go directly to the one who has harmed you.*

"If another member of the church sins against you, go and point out the fault when the two of you are alone. If the member listens to you, you have regained that one" (Matthew 18:15). As Peterson paraphrases it, "work it out between the two of you." Is this the way we usually respond to harm in the church or in the world? When we are harmed or feel harmed, we often avoid speaking directly to the person who harmed us. Instead, we speak to as many other people as possible. We want them on our side. With electronic communication, we can send an e-mail to everyone in the world except the person with whom we need to talk. Many of us have been on the receiving end of these calls and e-mails as people want to get us on their side in a dispute. This problem is especially acute for leaders. Persons attempt to get the pastor or lay leader on their side. This is called "triangulation." People want to make their problems your problem.

As leaders and friends, the first question to the person who is trying to triangulate you into their problem is: Have you spoken to the other person directly? If that person has not gone directly to the other, encourage him or her to do so. If the response is that he or she does not know how to do this, then your role can be to help support him or her in doing so, to coach him or her in the attitudes, skills and processes necessary for success. Your role is not to go with that person, unless there is an issue of safety or a significant imbalance of power. In those situations, it is helpful to seek some assistance from those with additional expertise.

"If the member listens to you, you have regained that one," or, as paraphrased by Peterson, "If he listens, you have made a friend" (Matthew 18:15).[60] You see here the connection with the shepherd and the lost sheep. What does it mean to listen and to be heard? What does it mean to be heard in a way that leads to regaining the brother or the sister, with being reconciled? Listening is the key to all conflict transformation and a key spiritual practice. Listening involves more than the simple act of hearing and understanding what is being said to you. In the Bible, listening also means responding to what you have heard by attempting to address the harm you have created. Responding by making things right is the sure sign that you have listened, heard and understood. Listening is about healing and restoration of the person harmed — and the regaining of the brother or sister.

Listening is encouraged by the way we speak our truth in love. If we simply practiced going directly at an early stage of a conflict, most conflicts would be resolved. But some people are hard of hearing. You have experienced this. Jesus recognizes this, and has a second suggestion.

- *Bring witnesses or third parties with you.*
"But if you are not listened to, take one or two others along with you, so that every word may be confirmed by the evidence of two or three witnesses" (Matthew 18:16). Here, Jesus suggests that the presence of others can help people listen (see Deuteronomy 19:15 and 1 Timothy 5:19). How can the witnesses or third parties help? Peterson suggests one answer in his paraphrasing, "If he won't listen, take one or two others along so that the presence of witnesses will keep things honest, and try again." These witnesses are not witnesses for one side or the other. They are present to assist both parties in the listening and hearing so that it is honest and productive. In practicing mediation, we are always amazed at how helpful a third party can be to two people in conflict. We have seen how a third party can provide a safe space for people to tell their stories. The third party helps both parties feel empowered to tell their stories as well as to listen to the other's story. The third party can help people move from their positions to their needs and interests, helping everyone work to address one another's needs and interests. Good things happen. Mediation works in a significant percentage of cases. However, Jesus recognizes that sometimes the assistance of one or two others does not result in the necessary listening and response, so Jesus suggests a third way.

- *Tell it to the church.*
"If the member refuses to listen to them, tell it to the church" (Matthew 18:17). What does this mean? Remembering that this is a process informed by the parable of the lost sheep, we see the church members as advocates for

good listening, hearing, accountability and healing: restoration to the community. Ideally, we imagine the church as a circle of healing and accountability. If the church "takes sides" or makes a premature judgment, the process will break down. Ultimately, the church might be called on to make a decision if the parties themselves cannot agree, including recognizing the decisions of those who have by their actions excluded themselves from community. Such decisions are recognized in heaven.

"Truly I tell you, whatever you bind on earth will be bound in heaven, and whatever you loose on earth will be loosed in heaven. Again, truly I tell you, if two of you agree on earth about anything you ask, it will be done for you by my Father in heaven" (Matthew 18:18-19).

These decisions regarding life in community are seen as critically important and are sacred decisions with power. These decisions are affirmed by God. Here we see the importance of community and actions that restore community.

Even with the church trying to assist, Jesus recognizes that sometimes this attempt fails as well, as the person does not listen. So Jesus makes a further suggestion.

- *Treat as Gentiles and tax collectors.*
"If he refuses to listen even to the church, let him be to you as a Gentile and a tax collector," or, as stated by Peterson, "If he won't listen to the church, you'll have to start over from scratch, confront him with the need for repentance, and offer again God's forgiving love" (Matthew 18:17). At times, the church has read this as support for excommunicating or excluding the one who fails to listen. Peterson's paraphrase recognizes that one who does not listen is not being excommunicated by the church. He or she has excommunicated himself or herself and is still in need of repentance. This translation is consistent with the way Jesus treated Gentiles and tax collectors. Jesus ate with them and spent significant time in their company. It is also consistent with what Jesus tells Peter about forgiveness. Since the person has excommunicated himself or herself by his or her failure to listen, you might decide, as

a leader, that you do not need to spend significant amounts of your time and energy trying to get him or her to listen. However, to follow Jesus, periodically you might want to try to meet for coffee or lunch where you can help offer again God's forgiving love and help him or her understand the need to be reconciled and restored into the community of the body.

- *Offer unlimited forgiveness.*

"Then Peter came and said to him, 'Lord, if another member of the church sins against me, how often should I forgive? As many as seven times?" Jesus said to him, "Not seven times, but, I tell you, seventy-seven times'" (Matthew 18:21-22, Thomas Nelson Bible). Peter thinks he is being generous. The Hebrew Bible says forgive three times. Isn't seven times greater? But Jesus says to Peter, You don't get it: seventy times seven. In other words, forgiveness should be unlimited. Here we see the movement of the Bible from Lamech's revenge "seventy-seven fold" (Genesis 4:24, Thomas Nelson Bible) to unlimited forgiveness of seventy times seven. We will address forgiveness in greater depth in Chapter 6.

- *Accept this Reality: If you do not forgive, you are not able to experience forgiveness.*

Jesus then tells the parable of the debtor who is forgiven a great debt, but who refuses to forgive the person who owes him a small amount of money.

> Then his lord summoned him and said to him, "You wicked slave! I forgave you all that debt because you pleaded with me. Should you not have had mercy on your fellow-slave, as I had mercy on you?" And in anger his lord delivered him to be tortured, until he should pay his entire debt. (Matthew 18:32-34)

Jesus goes on to say, "So also my heavenly Father will also do to every one of you, if you do not forgive your brother or sister from your heart" (Matthew 18:35).

Does this jar you? What does this mean? First of all, it means that not forgiving has consequences. This is SERIOUS BUSINESS. This is how the world is created. In the Lord's Prayer we ask to be forgiven as we forgive our debts or trespasses. Our forgiving is critical to our ability to receive forgiveness. We know we were forgiven before we are asked to forgive and that God's mercy and forgiveness is always open to us. However, when we close our heart to forgiving another, we close our heart to receiving the forgiveness offered to us.

This is not to say we are coerced to forgive. This is not cheap grace and cannot be manipulated. Forgiveness is always a gift from one person to another, which is primarily a gift to oneself, freeing ourselves from the thrall of the offense. The journey to forgiveness does not have a script. Each person who is harmed must pursue this journey at her or his own pace. The person harmed, the victim, sets the agenda.

However, we hear in this scripture a word similar to that of Bishop Tutu, when he titles his book *No Future Without Forgiveness*. Jesus has taught us the only way out of the cycles of woundedness, retribution and violence is through forgiveness.

PATH OF THE ONE WHO HARMS

The path of the one who harms is the path of moral accountability or responsibility. It involves conversion or *metanoia*. This path is a way to healing and restoration. We will go through the next stages more quickly as we have touched on all of this. This is the offender's response to the person harmed.

- Listen to what the person harmed has to say.
- Understand what harm you have created.
- Acknowledge (confess) that you understand the harm you have created.
- Repent for this harm by trying to make things right.

This is about real accountability. In the beginning the person harmed might want your eye or your hand, but what they ultimately need is real accountability, your doing those things through restitution and restoration that work toward making things right, toward healing. An example is the man who testified before the Truth and Reconciliation Commission in South Africa. He confessed his role in destroying a village but said he would spend the rest of his life helping to rebuild it.

• *Pursue healing and restoration.*
There is nothing retributive about this journey. This is not a punishment system. It is a system of real accountability, in a way that is healing. It is ultimately about restoration to community.

• *Do not harm.*
Here Jesus is telling us not to repeat harmful conduct. We are to be a new creation where we no longer do those things that destroy neighborliness, like abuse and exploitation.

• *Be like a child, as discussed earlier.*

• *Accept this Reality: If you do not follow this path, you will not enter the Kingdom of God.*
"Truly, I say to you, unless you change and become like children, you will never enter the kingdom of heaven," or as paraphrased by Peterson, "I'm telling you once and for all, that unless you return to square one and start over like children, you're not even going to get a look at the kingdom, let alone get in" (Matthew 18:3). (See also Mark 10:15 and Luke 18:17.) If this path is not followed, you will not enter the kingdom of heaven. Again, this is SERIOUS BUSINESS. How serious is this? "But if you give them [children] a hard time, bullying or taking advantage of their simple trust, you'll soon wish you hadn't. You'd be better off dropped in the middle of the lake with a millstone around your neck. Doom to the world for giving those God-believing children a hard time! Hard times are inevitable, but you don't have to make it worse — and it's doomsday to you if you do" (Matthew 18:6-7, Peterson).[61]

The door to the Kingdom is always open. Jesus is still ready to eat with you. The reality is that you cannot see the door, or the table, if you are not willing to follow the journey described.

> Woe to the world because of stumbling blocks! Occasions for stumbling are bound to come, but woe to the one by whom the stumbling block comes! If your hand or your foot causes you to stumble, cut it off and throw it away; it is better for you to enter life maimed or lame than to have two hands or two feet and to be thrown into the eternal fire. And if your eye causes you to stumble, tear it out and throw it away; it is better for you to enter life with one eye than to have two eyes and to be thrown into the hell of fire. (Matthew 18:7-9)

We need to cut out that portion of our lives that is getting in the way of our experiencing the Kingdom, whether it is idolatry involving money, sex or possessions — whatever distracts you from the love of God and neighbor. An exercise that you can do for yourself is to write down on paper what you feel you need to cut out of your life, put the paper in an envelope, and periodically open the envelope to evaluate how you are doing.

Unless we follow this journey of conversion, the cycles of woundedness, retribution and violence continue. We live in a very retributive, punishing world. We are asked by Jesus to follow another way.

Here in Matthew 18 we find a different journey than the journey of retributive justice. We find restorative justice as the way we are called to live as followers of Jesus. The journey of restorative justice, a subject we explore in Chapter 7, is the journey of reconciliation.

Exercise

The church of the first four centuries took seriously Jesus' admonition in the Sermon on the Mount. Before coming to the Eucharist, the early Christians followed the dictates of this scripture.[62]

"So when you are offering your gift at the altar, if you remember that

key guideposts on
the journey

we now turn to look at guideposts for the journey,
recognizing that our journeys of reconciliation
are not the same for every individual or community.

your brother or sister has something against you, leave your gift there before the altar and go; first be reconciled to your brother or sister, and then come and offer your gift" (Matthew 5: 23-24).

The following is an exercise created by Walter Wink that is based on this scripture. It is a silent exercise.

Now, what I'd like to suggest is that we act this scene out, each individually. Find a space somewhere and make for yourself an imaginary or makeshift altar. Actually visualize it as being in a certain spot. . . . Then physically walk through the act of bringing your gift to the altar, and there remember someone who has something against you, or if this is what comes to you, someone whom you have something against. Leave the gift before the altar and go to another part of your space, get two chairs, and place them opposite each other. Sit in one chair and be yourself; say what you need to say to the other person, imagined as being in the other chair. Then sit in the other person's chair and be that person, answering yourself as that person might. You'll be amazed at how real their answers will be. But don't just rehash the grievance. Have a conversation that will actually move the relationship toward reconciliation. We are trying deliberately to visualize and verbalize the actual possibility of reconciliation. Keep moving back and forth from one chair to the other till you have reached reconciliation, or at least have gone as far in that direction as you can. Then go back to the altar and offer your gift. If chairs are not available, try standing in two different places. But by all means *change positions* as you change roles. Otherwise the dialogue will become hopelessly muddied. Take about twenty minutes, and then come back together. (If space is limited, people can just spread out in sight of each other and do the exercise in silence, ignoring one another. Share afterward. If some people now feel that the next step is for them actually to initiate a dialogue with the other person, they might contract with one other person in the group to do so within a certain time and to report back, as an added incentive not to put it off indefinitely.)[63]

Concluding Ritual

Conclude with a passing of the peace that uses the Indonesian greeting, where you place your left hand over your heart as you shake hands with your right hand. The leader will do this with the person on the left and then one at a time the peace will be silently passed around the room, until it comes back to the leader who will say after receiving it, "Go in peace."

Notes

52. Eugene Peterson, *The Message Remix, The Bible in Contemporary Language* (Colorado Springs: NAVPRESS, 2003), p. 1455.

53. See also Mark 9:36, 10:15, 43-44; Luke 9:38, 18:17; John 3:3-5.

54. Marianne Williamson, *A Return to Love: Reflections on the Principles of A Course in Miracles* (New York: Harper Collins Publishers, 1975), p. 165.

55. Walter Wink, *The Powers That Be* (New York: Doubleday, 1998), p. 39.

56. Peterson, op. cit., p. 1455.

57. Martin Buber, *I and Thou*, trans. Walter Kaufmann (New York: Charles Scribner's Sons, 1970), p. 18.

58. Reinhold Niebuhr, *The Nature and Destiny of Man: A Christian Interpretation: Human Nature.* (Louisville: Westminster John Knox Press, 1996), p. 182.

59. Peterson, loc. cit., p. 1455.

60. Peterson, loc. cit., p. 1455.

61. Peterson, loc. cit., p. 1455.

62. Taylor Burton-Edward, "The Teaching of Peace in Early Christian Liturgies," master's thesis, Associated Mennonite Biblical Seminary, 1997.

63. Walter Wink, *Transforming Bible Study: A Leader's Guide* (Nashville: Abingdon Press, 1980), pp. 64-65.

Chapter 4

the importance of grieving and confronting our fears

the witness of the women at the foot of the cross and at the scene of the resurrection

Meanwhile, standing near the cross of Jesus were his mother, and his mother's sister, Mary the wife of Clopas, and Mary Magdalene. When Jesus saw his mother and the disciple whom he loved standing beside her, he said to his mother, "Woman, here is your son." Then he said to the disciple, "Here is your mother." And from that hour the disciple took her into his own home.

—John 19:25b-27

From noon on, darkness came over the whole land until three in the afternoon. And about three o'clock Jesus cried with a loud voice, "Eli, Eli, lema sabachthani?" that is, "My God, my God, why have you forsaken me?"

—Matthew 27:45-46

"Woman, why are you weeping? Whom are you looking for?" Supposing him to be the gardener, she said to him, "Sir, if you have carried him away, tell me where you have laid him, and I will take him away." Jesus said to her, "Mary!" She turned and said to him in Hebrew, "Rabbouni!" (which means Teacher).

—John 20:15-16

After the sabbath, as the first day of the week was dawning, Mary Magdalene and the other Mary went to see the tomb. And suddenly there was a great earthquake; for an angel of the Lord, descending from heaven, came and rolled back the stone and sat on it. His appearance was like lightning, and his clothing white as snow. For fear of him the guards shook and became like dead men. But the angel said to the women, "Do not be afraid; I know that you are looking for Jesus who was crucified. He is not here; for he has been raised as he said. Come, see the place where he lay. Then go quickly and tell his disciples, 'He has been raised from the dead, and indeed he is going ahead of you to Galilee; there you will see him.' This is my message for you." So they left the tomb quickly with fear and great joy, and ran to tell his disciples.

—Matthew 28:1-8

Preparation

- Read the following texts related to the cross and the empty tomb: John 19:25-27, John 20:1-18, Matthew 27:45-56 and Matthew 28:1-10.
- In your journal write all of the questions you have about these texts as well as your own reflections.
- Spend some time with your questions, letting these questions go deeper and deeper. Note your insights.
- Look at the questions we have asked and write down your thoughts as to where these questions lead you, which may include other questions.
- Spend some time with the text and your journaling before you turn to the reflections that follow.
- After you have read the Reflection section, write down in your journal other insights and questions you have.

Setup

A small round table is in the middle of the room with a circle of chairs around the table. On the table is a single candle and perhaps a stone, a small crucifix or strand of prayer beads. Some light refreshments are in the room. Consider using one of these objects as a talking piece.

Centering

The leader welcomes everyone as the candle is lighted.

Remembrance

As we gather, let us remember: "The eternal God is your dwelling place, and underneath are the everlasting arms" (Deuteronomy 33:27a).

Hymn

"Stay With Us"   (**TFWS #2199**)

Prayer of Lamentation

Let us pray silently, lifting up to God any present grief or fear we're experiencing. (After a time of silence, the leader closes with "Amen.")

Words of Assurance

As we begin to reflect together on the role of grieving and facing our fears, let us read together, as if for the first time, Psalm 23.

Psalm 23   (**UMH #754**)

> The Lord is my shepherd, I shall not want.
> The Lord makes me lie down in green pastures;
>> leads me beside still waters;
>> restores my soul.
>> leads me in right paths
>> for the sake of the Lord's name.

Even though I walk through the darkest valley,
> I fear no evil;
> for you are with me;
> your rod and your staff,
> they comfort me.

You prepare a table before me
> in the presence of my enemies;
> you anoint my head with oil;
> my cup overflows.

Surely; goodness and mercy; shall follow me
> all the days of my life,
> and I shall dwell in the house of the Lord
> as long as I live.

The leader tests consensus on using the small crucifix or strand of prayer beads or small stone as a talking piece.

Relational Covenant

The leader reminds everyone of the relational covenant that is posted on the wall. The covenant is read, and everyone affirms his or her commitment to the covenant.

Reading of the Text

The leader indicates that the context for the first readings is the crucifixion of Jesus. A volunteer reads John 19:25-27, then Matthew 27:45-56. The leader invites silent reflection. Following the brief silence a volunteer reads John 20:1-18 and Matthew 28:1-10.

Questions

Leader: What follows are just some suggested questions to help you formulate questions for group discussion. We would suggest having four or
five questions prepared. Others will flow from the conversation. After each
question you ask, use the talking piece passed around the Circle to the left,
to hear all of the voices as participants respond to the question. Then hold
the talking piece so that the conversation can flow naturally, building on
what has been said. When you get to the second question, follow the same
practice with the talking piece.

- For you, what is the significance of the women, including Mary the
  mother of Jesus, Mary Magdalene and others remaining at or near the
  cross and then going to the tomb? What about the disciples (men) who
  went home or the soldiers who pretended to be stricken?
- Jesus at his death says, "My God, why have you forsaken me?" Have you
  experienced being forsaken, being abandoned?
- Why is grieving our loss, whatever that loss is, so important in our
  journey of reconciliation?
- Jesus speaks to his mother and the beloved disciple from the cross. What
  do you hear in these statements, "Behold, your son" and "Behold your
  mother?"
- How is naming our fears important in our journey?
- How can we come to believe the words of the angel, "Do not be afraid,"
  in our moments of trauma, fear and grief?

| REFLECTION | THE IMPORTANCE OF GRIEVING AND CONFRONTING OUR FEARS |

*These reflections are to stimulate your own thinking, not to limit the possible
interpretations and the finding of what is meaningful to you in the passages.*

THE CONTEXT OF DEATH AND ABANDONMENT

"My God, my God, why have you forsaken me?" In Jesus' own cry of abandonment we are confronted with the loss and fear felt also by his own mother and those followers close to him. Those near the cross face the pain and loss of one they love, the loss of life as they know it and the fear of not being able to proceed with living. Seeing violent taunts to Jesus, those gathered by him mourn the loss of human dignity and the fear of ongoing abandonment.

The Context of the Women

In all four gospels, women kept vigil at the death of Jesus and women came early in the morning to the place where Jesus was laid and where they find the empty tomb. Women remained a constant presence at or near this deathly scene when others scattered and even hid in their homes. These women teach us about courage, the courage to face our fears, and they teach us the importance of grieving.

In order to appreciate the power of the witness in these two gospels, we should remember that the gospels of John and Matthew were written at a time of conflict and hostility — between Jews of the synagogue and those who followed the Messiah in Matthew and among Jewish Christians and Gentile Christians in John. We will discuss this in greater detail in Chapter 8. Those who received these gospels, the followers of Jesus, were experiencing this ongoing trauma. Some families were estranged and reprisals could be violent in the face of institutional powers threatened by the new community of Jesus. In her commentary on John, Gail O'Day describes the followers' painful choice of remaining with the synagogue (and denying their beliefs) or "being forced to leave the synagogue and the community that had nurtured them and given them life" by claiming Jesus as the Messiah.[64] "The intensity of the language around the use of 'The Jews' is fraught with the pain of this choice."[65] We know this text in John's gospel as well as others have been misused to express anti-Semitic views, and we believe that it is very important to understand that this is an internal community tension within the Christian community between Jewish Christians and Gentile Christians. It is in the face of this fear and mourning that we see the importance to the early Christians of the women bearing witness at the foot of the cross and at the scene of the resurrection.

The Challenge of Living in Holy Saturday

It was a small one-room church in a rural farm setting for this funeral, a service of death and resurrection for a family friend, and the slightly warm humid day seemed to rest on us like a pall. Family and friends were gathering for the tragic loss of a beloved father, brother, uncle and friend. All was quiet as persons paid their respects and offered condolences, making their way through a receiving line at the open door entrance to the church. The casket was open for viewing as mourners passed by. Just prior to the start of the funeral, with family gathered around the deceased for prayer, the grieving widow, tears streaming down her face, leaned into the casket to gently kiss her beloved husband of 60 years. A gasp among those gathered was audible; it was almost as if this were a scandalous gesture on her part. Her sons pulled her away as the casket was tightly closed and sealed and then guided her to the front pew. Soft cries and murmurs of concern swelled up in the room. A few wails erupted. I, Stephanie, thought at that moment how varied our rituals and practices are in times of grief and loss. And, I thought about how some of us have been formed in practices that seemingly try to insulate us from the reality of death and suffering. How do we respond to trauma, suffering and death, which are part of everyone's lives? How can we live through these events in a way that is ultimately healing?

In many traditions, women not only usher in new life at birth but also are stewards of funeral rites and customs at death. Funerary rites such as cleansing, perfuming, grave clothes (John 20:7) and other preparations are signs of honor for those who have died. Some practices such as wailing and songs of lament give expression to this loss. For some of us a loss can be so deep it is like injury to our body and our very cells cry out in lament. Still others experience real trauma to their body and soul and a loss so deep and pervasive that its "deathness" continues to confront in every present moment. This is the experience of Holy Saturday. Holy Saturday is that day between Good Friday and Easter — that time between the death of Jesus and the witness of the resurrection. As an Easter people, Christians today know that Holy Saturday moves to Easter; however, there are times of loss, trauma and grief in our lives when the "deathness" of Holy Saturday pervades. The challenge for us may be how to remain for a time in Holy Saturday — bearing witness to the loss, the pain and the grief of harm, trauma or death.

What happens in that time between Jesus' death on the cross and his rising on Sunday morning — the time of waiting and tending to grief and loss for the women? The quaking of the earth in Matthew points to the cosmic nature of Jesus' journey — the descent to hell on Holy Saturday. From ancient hymns and liturgies we see the witness of our God who knows hell and breaks the power of its bondage.

> I am your God, who for your sake have become your son. Out of love for you and your descendants I now by my own authority command all who are held in bondage to come forth, all who are in darkness to be enlightened, all who are sleeping to arise. I order you, O sleeper, to awake. I did not create you to be held a prisoner in Hell. Rise from the dead, for I am the life of the dead. Rise up, work of my hands, you who were created in my image. Rise, let us leave this place, for you are in Me and I in you; together we form one person and cannot be separated.[66]

Those who have experienced trauma, whether in the atrocities of war, genocide, sexual abuse, earthquake or other tragedy know the bondage of hell on this earth — that which grips the body and soul and creates a crisis. In her research and writing on trauma and healing, Shelly Rambo suggests, "Trauma, in my view, is not only an experience of encountering death. Trauma is really located in the crisis of surviving that death," Rambo says. "There's suffering in living beyond a death and not yet being able to see life."[67]

In many Christian practices, Holy Saturday is that awkward day between Good Friday and Easter that we skip too readily to experience the promise of new life. What we learn from the witness of the women is the importance of remaining for a time in Holy Saturday, tending to our grief, mourning our loss and bearing witness to the tragedy and suffering. These are critical aspects of the journey toward healing, reconciliation and restorative justice — yes, even toward Easter.

The Experience and Witness of the Women

In John, Mary the mother of Jesus, her sister Mary the wife of Clopas, and Mary Magdalene stayed at the foot of the cross, staying with Jesus and their grief, not running away. In Matthew, we are told, many women stayed at the foot of the cross.

For John, the words of Jesus to his mother and the beloved disciple, "Behold your son" and "Behold your mother" (John 19:25-27) direct our attention to the loss of Jesus, the child of this earthly mother, and to the intimacy of family and relationships. It is a real human death. Jesus knew what a loss this would be for his mother and for the beloved disciples and those who followed him. He knew she needed a son and he (the beloved disciple) needed a mother. Jesus knew that we all need companions and community as we walk "through the darkest valley." These words uttered by Jesus in his last breaths were not only comforting to those grieving but also serve as a sign of hope for a continued future to those who followed him closely. Mary, the mother of Jesus, who was present throughout his earthly ministry and is now close by his side at his death will be with the beloved disciple and other brothers and sisters as they bear witness to their loss and grief and tell the stories of life with Jesus. With Jesus' words, his mother and his disciples find a safe, relational place together to mourn, to face their fears and continue the ministry.

In Matthew, Jesus' death is marked by a tumultuous earthquake (Matthew 28:2): "And suddenly there was a great earthquake; for an angel of the Lord, descending from heaven, came and rolled back the stone and sat on it." It is as John Mogabgab describes, cosmic and spiritual: "The rock-hewn tomb becomes a womb of a New Creation. . . . The transformation of all things underway. And yet, what a valley of tears continues to separate the old creation from the new. What perverse resiliency resides in all that harms, separates, angers or saddens us. How tragic a gap yawns between glimpses of all that we hope for and the luminous fulfillment of our hope."[68]

The tragic gap is revealed in the lament of Jesus himself on the cross. Here Jesus confronts his and our deepest fear: abandonment by God and others. For Tom it was a deeply spiritual experience with colleagues Buddhist, Muslim, Jewish and Christian lawyers and professors during a visit with persons in the Focolare movement in Italy that gave rise to new insight. Chiara Lubich and other Catholic women developed a laywomen's movement in bomb shelters in 1943 during the bombing of Trent. In reading the Bible, they determined that Jesus' prayer in John for unity meant unity of all people, all creation (John 17:21). At the core of this unity is seeing the face and heart of Jesus forsaken in the lives of each human being. In doing so we are in solidarity with the greatest suffering and pain that Jesus experienced and that humanity experiences: feeling abandoned by God. "My God, my God, why have you forsaken me?" (Matthew 27:46).

In that cry, the incarnate God, present on the cross, most fully identifies with our human condition: alienation from God and neighbor. Here is the common ground for our unity, for the deepest love for God, Jesus and for humanity. On the cross we see it all come together — the violence, the response to Jesus by the principalities and the powers, and the experience in the midst of the violence of feeling abandoned by God and neighbor.

Here we stand in the tragic gap — that chasm between what we hoped for and the realization of those hopes. What is tragic in that gap is that perverse resiliency resid[ing] in all that harms, separates, angers or saddens. Loss, pain, suffering and violence seem all too ready to revisit us and trauma too eager to cycle back to us in real ways. We may be more inclined to run home like the disciples or be buried in a trance like the Roman soldiers in the face of suffering, violence and death. We may get stuck in Holy Saturday — incessantly revisited by death, pain and trauma and seemingly unable to imagine life beyond this earthly "hell." We need to follow the witness of the women at the cross and then at the tomb in mourning and facing our fears, essential to being able to experience the healing and hope of Easter Sunday.

"Mary [Magdalene] stood weeping outside the tomb. As she wept, she bent over to look into the tomb: and she saw two angels. . . . They said to her, 'Woman, why are you weeping?'" (John 20:11). Mary, first addressed as "woman" by the angels, fears that the body of Jesus has been stolen. She then turns toward Jesus, not knowing him, who addresses her, "Woman, why are you weeping?" In her confusion, she expresses her fear again, and Jesus addresses her by name. "Mary!" She turns again to him in response, "Rabbouni (Teacher)," a term of relationship and familiarity. Jesus immediately admonishes her not to hold on to him as he has not yet ascended. Rather, he tells her to "go to my brothers and say to them, 'I am ascending to my Father and your Father, to my God and your God.'" Mary went and told them these things. It was later that day when Jesus appears to the disciples with the assurance of the Spirit (paraclete): "Peace be with you" (John 20:19).

Though the use of the masculine "Father" for God can be painful and troublesome for some in this passage, it speaks to the intimacy and familial relationship with the disciples. This is a comforting promise for the continuation of community in the midst of ruptured family and relationships. Just as Mary, the mother of Jesus, points to this continued family and witness, the women, Mary Magdalene in particular, give witness to the continuation of this earthly ministry experienced though Jesus.

There is still much that is not known, and a mix of joy and fear is present with the women as described in Matthew. This tragic gap is not so easily traversed. Holy Saturday is real and present for some time.

Shelly Rambo, in her exploration of trauma and Holy Saturday indicates that "The distinctively Johannine vocabulary of 'remaining' does not simply mark a vacuum; instead, it forges a place of witness between death and life, figured in the paraclete spirit. . . . This 'remaining' spirit persists between

death and life, hinging the two in a fragile but powerful relationship. . . .
This Saturday Spirit does not erase the sting of death. The Spirit is, rather,
the breath on which an Easter proclamation must be carried."[69]

THE IMPORTANCE OF GRIEVING AND FACING OUR FEARS IN THE JOURNEY OF RECONCILIATION

Why is grieving so important? Not grieving the trauma often pushes it deep
in our psyche where we medicate it with, for example, drugs or alcohol. It
can create numbness and isolation. Suppressing grief can create a volcanic
mix of anger and emotions that erupt in destructive ways. The other tragic
reality is that those harmed can become those who then harm others.
Cycles of woundedness, retribution and violence are repeated.

We cannot heal what we cannot feel. We need time to feel our pain and
loss and all of the emotions and tears that surround them. As we mourn
and grieve we start the journey of healing the wound. It is important to our
healing that these laments are heard by others who are willing to acknowledge, attend to, recognize and respect our loss.

We know that mourning provides a way to integrate our losses into our
lives. It is essential for the journey of healing and reconciliation within us
and in our communities. This journey has many rhythms — whether weeping and wailing with dances and shouts or tending to details of burial rites,
or prayerfully writing out our hearts in our journal, or exercising vigorously
to release rage and pain — these and many more are expressions of lament
and mourning. As the early church began to tell and retell the events of the
death, burial and resurrection of Jesus, the power and hope took root.

Finding a place of safety is important in being able to deal with our grief
and our fears, as Jesus recognized with his mother and the beloved disciple. A few women in the Wajir district in the northeastern part of Kenya
wanted to make sure that the market was safe for anyone to buy and sell in
order to feed their children. Wajir at the time of the mid-1990s was experiencing increased clan-based conflict and a flow of refugees from Somalia

and Ethiopia. During a night when gunfire erupted Dekha was holding her child under the bed. As she held her own child, she heard her mother tell the story of holding Dekha in safety under the bed some 30 years ago. Dekha decided to reach out to other women. Lamenting the violence, the trafficking of guns, the fear of rape and abuse facing their children, they decided to create a safe zone for the market. Using their personal connections, they eventually worked with elders from the clans and enabled the war to stop for a period.[70] Without refuge, a safe house, a sense of relative security, we are prone to react to perceived danger — to fight, flee, hide or deny our loss and fear. Dekha and her women friends created such a place of safety.

Affirming ourselves as beloved children of God is important in dealing with our grief and our fears. For Cheryl, the words during the morning ritual at the shelter for women and children became her sense of security and safety within herself. Somehow looking in the mirror each morning and repeating, "You are a beloved child of God" clothed her with what was required to face another day toward recovery and healing for her and her children. She said them again and again standing in front of the mirror at the beginning of each day. She showered those words on her children. It had been a couple of weeks since she had left the home she shared with her husband and their son and daughter. She wondered aloud to herself now why she had not left sooner. She was confused by what she heard from the pastor — that she should try to work on this marriage, that her husband was after all the head of the household, and that perhaps her willful behavior was contributing to his violent outbursts. But the drinking was getting worse, and though she loved him, she feared for her safety and that of her children. She finally turned to a friend in the congregation who connected her with the women's shelter. She was not at all certain what the future would hold, but for the time being, she and her children were in a safe place.

Giving voice and witness to our stories and experiences of harm and trauma is important in dealing with the unspeakable, the isolation, the silence, the fear and shame. It is also important to our healing that our stories are heard, acknowledged and respected by others. In the next chapter we will deal in greater depth with the importance of telling our stories and restorying our lives. There is much loss in our world related to trauma, to violence, abuse and atrocities perpetrated on humanity and God's creation.

Trauma and woundedness not touched in some restorative way can become the source of reenacted trauma. Here is where we find hope in the practices of restorative justice — addressing harm, real accountability and the engagement between those harmed and those perpetrating harm. Breaking those cycles of violence is critical to our healing and wholeness as a community.

As we continue to explore the journey of forgiveness, restorative justice and reconciliation, we have found the diagram on the following page helpful. This visual was created by Olga Botcharova from lessons learned from her work in dealing with violence and the trauma of war and atrocities in the former Yugoslavia. As you can see, there is an inner circle that cycles from aggression back to aggression. It begins with injury, pain, shock, denial and realization of the loss. It includes suppression of our grief and our fears, being stuck in our anger and the question of "why me?" leading to a desire for revenge. In the process we create myths and heroes and the "right conflict history" in order to justify our own aggression. Olga realized that the only way to break out of this cycle of violence and retribution is to begin with mourning, expressing our grief, accepting our loss and confronting our fears. In the next chapter we will try to understand the remainder of her diagram, starting with naming our loss and our fears through confronting the other.

One of the issues we face on the journey is whether the person harmed, for their own healing, can or should, as in Matthew 18, confront the person or persons who harmed them. What do you think of what Christopher Marshall, the New Testament scholar from New Zealand, writes?

From Agression to Reconciliation[71]

Because they are bound together to the event, both victim and offender need each other to experience the liberation and healing from the continuing thrall of the offense. The offender needs the victim to trigger or sharpen his contrition, to hear his confession, remit his guilt, and to affirm his ability to start fresh. The victim needs the offender to hear her pain, answer her questions, absorb her resentment, and affirm her dignity. Each holds the key to the other's liberation."[72]

We have come to know the importance of being attentive to the specific needs and desires of those who are harmed, knowing that only they can decide whether to take any of these steps in the previous diagram, including whether to meet with the person who harmed them.

Let me, Stephanie, tell you one story as a bridge to the next chapter. I was not at all convinced that Julia should participate in a community meeting with Howard, a convicted sex offender who had raped her as a girl. Nearing the end of his prison term, Howard wished to return to the community where he had lived for 50 years. His elderly parents were members of the same congregation as Julia and her family. Julia, now an adult leader in the community, was insistent that this meeting was the only way to address the deep fears of having Howard present in the places of her life and work and her family's life and faith.

Although I knew that Howard had pursued an authentic path of accountability and transformation, this did not quell my anxiety about repeating patterns of abuse and potential for revictimization. Nevertheless, I trusted Julia and her determination of what would be most helpful. We considered together the "what ifs?" related to such engagement. Julia explored the nature and details of the meeting with her support network and with local authorities. Her journey of healing and transformation had included hard grief and trauma work. She was confident that she wanted to name and negotiate her own terms of accountability and coexistence with Howard. After much preparation, there was agreement about how the meeting would be conducted and who would be present, including support persons and officials related to the decision making. The process involved a circle and took some time, but eventually all agreed to guidelines for interaction that included such things as education about the crime, transparency about the conviction, and the continued path of accountability. The circle established specific parameters regarding Howard's interaction with persons in the neighborhood and the congregation. For Julia, it was a powerful shift to be asking for what she wanted and needed rather than responding or reacting to others. These agreements were not entered into easily, and yet they marked a moment of reconciliation. No longer known only as victim and offender, Julia and Howard reentered this community with a new story.[73]

As we move through the next chapters we will explore more fully the journey of those harmed; those who perpetrate harm; the importance of truth-telling, restorying, and rehumanizing the "other"; and authentic paths of accountability and healing.

On the journey of reconciliation, forgiveness and restorative justice, the steadfast care of the women at the cross provides a space and time to grieve. Their faithfulness to face threat and fear gives us courage. Their turning toward the resurrected one and witness to the presence of Jesus even in the tragic confusion and "in-between-ness" gives us hope. For it is the God of abundant love, whose relationship with us cannot be destroyed and whose solidarity with our suffering enables us to face our own fears and perhaps embrace the suffering of others, even those who may seek to do us harm.

Exercise

- If your setting allows, prepare a space for walking prayer. It may be a garden or green space. You may set up a labyrinth or simply invite persons to walk within the meeting space.
- Place two tables near the edge of your meeting space; prepare them as areas for meditation and prayer.
- Assemble crosses, oils, spices, prayer beads and other elements that speak to the texts today.
- The leader invites persons into a time of prayer, moving through walking as they are able or sitting at a meditation table with friends to reflect on the following: "As I think about my journey of reconciliation, I feel these laments and fears speaking in my very muscles and bones. Walk with me, Jesus; help me not to be afraid." As I think about the world groaning toward wholeness, I sense the suffering, laments and fears of many in our world. "Walk with us, Jesus; help us not to be afraid."

After about 15 minutes, gather persons back in the Circle and invite them to share insights and reflections as they are comfortable and able to do so. Suggest that others thoughts might be added to their journal.

Concluding Ritual

This ritual is adapted from the repertoire of worship consultant Marcia McFee (www.marciamcfee.com).

The leader invites all to stand in a circle as they are able. German mystic Meister Eckhardt says, "Every creature is a word of God." With that in mind, I invite us to proclaim this of one another around the Circle. The leader turns to the person on her or his left and says, [Name], you are the Word of God. Everyone responds, "Thanks be to God!" Continue with that person then turning to her or his left and saying [Name], you are the Word of God. Everyone responds, "Thanks be to God" until the proclamation has moved completely around the Circle.

The leader then says, "Peace be with you."

Notes

64. Gail R. O'Day, "John," in *The Women's Bible Commentary*, eds. Carol Newsom and Sharon H. Ringe (Louisville: Westminster John Knox Press), p. 294.

65. Ibid.

66. Excerpts from the Second "Homily for Holy Saturday," Jacques-Paul Migne, *Patrologia Graeca*, Vol. 43 (Paris: Imprimerie Catholique,1864), pp. 462-63.

67. Karine Abalyan, "In Harm's Way: The Wide-Ranging Repercussions of War," *Boston University Research Magazine* (2009).

68. John Mogabgab, "Standing in the Tragic Gap," *Weavings: A Journal of the Christian Spiritual Life* (March/April 2009), p. 2.

69. Shelly Rambo, "Faith Facing Trauma," *Review & Expositor: A Quarterly Baptist Theological Journal*, Vol. 105, No. 2. See also Shelly Rambo, *Spirit and Trauma: A Theology of Remaining* (Louisville: Westminster John Knox Press, 2010), p. 229.

70. John Paul Lederach, *The Moral Imagination* (London: Oxford University Press, 2005), pp. 10-11.

71. Copyright 1998 by Olga Botcharova. Used by permission.

72. Christopher Marshall, *Beyond Retribution: A New Testament Vision for Justice, Crime and Punishment* (Grand Rapids: Wm. B. Eerdmans Publishing Co., 2001), p. 277.

73. This story was first shared by Stephanie Hixon in *Conflict and Communion: Reconciliation and Restorative Justice at Christ's Table*, ed. Thomas Porter (Nashville: Discipleship Resources, 2006), p. 94.

Chapter 5

truth-telling and the confrontation of the other

jesus and the canaanite woman and the story of naming the harm and giving bread at the last supper

Just then a Canaanite woman from that region came out and started shouting, "Have mercy on me, Lord, Son of David; my daughter is tormented by a demon." But he did not answer her at all. And his disciples came and urged him, saying, "Send her away, for she keeps shouting after us." He answered, "I was sent only to the lost sheep of the house of Israel." But she came and knelt before him, saying, "Lord, help me." He answered, "It is not fair to take the children's food and throw it to the dogs." She said, "Yes, Lord, yet even the dogs eat the crumbs that fall from their masters' table." Then Jesus answered her, "Woman, great is your faith! Let it be done for you as you wish." And her daughter was healed instantly.

—Matthew 15:22-28

When it was evening, he came with the twelve. And when they had taken their places and were eating, Jesus said, "Truly I tell you, one of you will betray me, one who is eating with me." . . . While they were eating, he took a loaf of bread, and after blessing it he broke it, gave it to them, and said, "Take; this is my body." Then he took a cup, and after giving thanks he gave it to them, and all of them drank from it.

—Mark 14:17-18, 22-23

Preparation

- Read Matthew 15:21-28 and Mark 14:17-24.
- In your journal write all of the questions you have about these texts as well as your own reflections. Spend some time with your questions, letting these questions go deeper and deeper. Note your insights.
- Then look at the questions we have asked and write down your thoughts as to where these questions lead you, which may include other questions.
- Spend some time with the text and your journaling before you turn to the reflections that follow.
- After you have read the Reflection section, write down in your journal other insights and questions you have.

Setup

A small round table is in the middle of the room with a circle of chairs around the table. On the table is a single candle as well as some pieces of bread in baskets. Some light refreshments are in the room. Consider using a talking stick as a talking piece. This can be a simple wooden stick. In some traditions, a talking stick reminds those in the Circle to speak truth and to speak with respect. It can be adorned with other elements, ones that speak to the themes of this session.

Centering

The leader welcomes everyone as the candle is lighted.

Responsive Reading

The One: In the singing, in the silence, in the hands expectant open,
            In the Presence at this table,

The Many: Jesus Christ be wine of grace.
            Jesus Christ be bread of peace.

The One: In the question, in the answer, in the moment of acceptance,
            In the heart's cry, in the healing, in the circle of your people,

The Many: Jesus Christ be wine of grace.
            Jesus Christ be bread of peace.

(Adapted from TFWS #2255)

Hymn
"Walls Mark our Bound'ries" (See Appendix E)

The Leader asks everyone if they are willing to use the talking stick as a talking piece.

Prayer
Let us pray together: "Dear God of all people and all nations, as we hold this talking stick, may we have the courage to name our truths and speak them with love and respect. Amen."

Relational Covenant
The leader reminds everyone of the relational covenant that is posted on the wall. The covenant is read, and everyone affirms his or her commitment to the covenant.

Reading of the Text

The leader invites someone to read aloud Matthew 15:21-28. The leader invites the group to a brief time of silence. Then the leader invites someone to read aloud the second text, Mark 14:17-24.

Questions

Leader: What follows are just some suggestions to help you formulate questions for group discussion. We would suggest having four or five questions prepared. Others will flow from the conversation. After each question you ask, use the talking piece passed around the Circle to the left, to hear all of the voices as participants respond to the question. Then hold the talking piece so that the conversation can flow naturally, building on what has been said. When you get to the second question, follow the same practice with the talking piece.

- The Canaanite woman persisted in finally transcending the social barriers between Israelites and Canaanites and getting attention from Jesus for her sick child. Was there a time that you acted urgently to get attention for a loved one? Have you crossed barriers, borders or boundaries in your journey?
- What moved Jesus to change his mission from only "the lost sheep of the house of Israel" to a mission that involved healing the daughter of a Canaanite?
- How have you experienced naming harm, truth-telling and confrontation of the other?
- What difference would it make in our communities if we were to come together regularly — not just on Sunday — around the Lord's Table and practice naming truth and harm and offering bread?

REFLECTION TRUTH-TELLING, NAMING THE HARM AND GIVING BREAD

These reflections are to stimulate your own thinking, not to limit the possible interpretations and the finding of what is meaningful to you in the passages.

TRUTH-TELLING AND THE CONFRONTATION OF THE OTHER

Just prior to this encounter with the Canaanite woman and the healing of her child, Jesus is again teaching and interpreting the laws in tension-filled exchanges with the scribes and Pharisees. He decides to get away, toward Tyre and Sidon, places outside of Israel typically identified with nonbelievers. It is Jesus who is approached by the Canaanite woman shouting for mercy. Her child is tormented by demons, gripped by some unexplainable sickness or disease. Jesus does not respond to her. The disciples urge Jesus to "send her away, for she keeps shouting after us" (Matthew 15:23). Weren't we trying to get away from all this? Didn't we just leave a place where you (Jesus) were given a really hard time?

What unfolds next is textured with location, history, language and custom. With what eyes and ears do we meet the text? There is beneath the surface an interplay of narratives — the deliverance of Israel and the conquest of Canaan. Those who identify with the liberation narrative may not so readily see the identification of others with a displaced indigenous people.[74] Jesus identifies himself and seemingly his ministry within the confines of Israel, sent to only "the lost sheep of the house of Israel." So, as a Canaanite, you are not among them, you are not "in my parish." In fact, the Canaanites along with the Hittites, Girgashites, Amorites, the Perizzites, the Hivites and the Jebusites were nations that the scriptures say God gave to Israel to defeat when entering the promised land (Deuteronomy 7:1-2). It is the Canaanite woman who offers words and gestures of respect and honor to Jesus, kneeling and addressing him as "Lord" — a sign of honor not always given Jesus by his own. These actions speak as loudly as her words: "Help me." Still, Jesus responds in language typical of his birth, his identity and upbringing,

"It is not fair to take the children's [referencing those of Israel] food and throw it to the dogs [referencing those outside of Israel]." To which the Canaanite woman replies, "Yes, Lord, yet even the dogs eat the crumbs that fall from their masters' table." In some ways it is a witty turn of phrase to which Jesus can now proclaim only, "Great is your faith!"

In this encounter Jesus not only sees and hears the Canaanite woman with new eyes and ears but we also see him transformed in his role and ministry. The child of the Canaanite woman is healed. Healings are no longer restricted to those of Israel. Jesus then speaks of having "compassion" for the crowd (Matthew 15:32) and feeds the crowd by filling baskets with broken leftover pieces. Compassion drives mission. In telling the truth and confronting the other, boundaries of status are shattered, borders of exclusion are transcended, harms woven into the fabric of one anothers histories are acknowledged, crowds are fed, and those not typically seen and heard are healed.

THE POWER OF THE CONFRONTATION AND THE NATURE OF THE OTHER

In Chapter 4 we recognized the importance of grieving and confronting our fears. We were "en-couraged" by the courage of the women near the cross and the tomb. Telling one's truth and confronting the other also takes courage, as we discussed in Chapter 3.

In our work, one of the most important lessons we have learned about healing and the journey of reconciliation is the importance of telling our stories. Telling one's story is important to the person harmed. Being able to give voice to the pain and have the story heard and acknowledged is essential. Telling the story in a place of safety, with all of its emotions and to people who truly listen and who acknowledge the pain is crucial to the healing and to one's ability to have the courage to confront the other.[75]

Telling the story to the one who did the harm, when the other acknowledges the pain and the truth of the story, is potentially liberating. Telling the story to one who did the harm is important for the healing journey of the one who created harm as well, as this is how the offender learns the truth of the harm. Offenders need to hear and understand the pain created by the harm and its whirlpool effect on others. Here the offender can begin to break through the denial, the justifications, the excuses, the victim blaming and minimization to see the humanity of the one who has been harmed. We see here the lessons Jesus taught us in Matthew 18 as we described in Chapter 3 about the moral authority of the one harmed to confront the other, hopefully leading to accountability and healing.

In the confrontation, in the engagement, the one harmed also has the opportunity to hear the story of the other. Henry Wadsworth Longfellow says, "If we could read the secret history of our enemies, we should find in each [person's] life sorrow and suffering enough to disarm all hostility."[76] This is why Olga Botcharova says we must move from the question "Why me?" to "Why them?" This is the only way out of seeing the other as the enemy who engenders destructive anger and a desire for revenge. Without excuses for the wrongdoing, we begin to see beneath the act or acts to the forces that created the act or acts. We begin to see the other as a human being with whom we are interconnected and interdependent.

The Canaanite woman insists on Jesus hearing her story. In the light of her experience under the domination of Israel, she is remarkable in the way she tells her story. Jesus hears the story and responds. He moves from "I was sent only to the lost sheep of the house of Israel," to "Woman, great is your faith! Let it be done for you as you wish." This is a healing moment for the daughter, for the mother, for Jesus, and symbolically and actually in that moment for Canaanites and Israelites.

John Paul Lederach relays an encounter between two representatives of conflicted ethnic groups in Ghana in the 1990s. A land dispute led to violence. He recounts:

> The Dagombas, a group with a sustained and powerful tradition of chieftaincy, have a social and leadership structure that loaned itself to negotiation with European slave traders. They were the most powerful and dominant group in the north of the country.

. . . The Konkombas, on the other hand, were more dispersed. Principally, agriculturalists, "yam growers," as they at times were denigrated and stereotyped . . . [t]hey were a non-chiefly tribe.

A small group of African mediators . . . began the process of creating space for dialogue between representatives of the two ethnic groups. . . . Given the tradition and rights afforded the highest chiefs, little could be done except to let the chief speak.

"Look at them," he said, addressing himself more to the mediators than the Konkombas. "Who are they even that I should be in this room with them. They do not even have a chief. Who am I to talk to? They are a people with nothing who have just come from the fields and now attack us in our own villages. They could have at least brought an old man. But look! They are just boys born yesterday."

The Konkomba spokesman asked to respond. Fearing the worst, the mediators provided him space to speak. The young man turned and addressed himself to the chief of the enemy tribe:

You are perfectly right, Father, we do not have a chief. We have not had one for years. You will not even recognize the man we have chosen to be our chief. And this has been our problem. The reason we react, the reason our people go on rampages and fights resulting in all these killings and destruction arises from this fact. We do not have what you have. It really is not about the town, or the land, or that market guinea fowl. I beg you, listen to my words, Father. I am calling you Father because we do not wish to disrespect you. You are a great chief. But what is left to us? Do we have no other means but this violence to receive in return the one thing we seek, to be respected and to establish our own chief who could indeed speak with you, rather than having a young boy do it on our behalf?

The attitude, tone of voice, and use of the word Father spoken by the young Konkomba man apparently so affected the chief that he sat for a moment without response. When finally he spoke, he did so with a changed voice, addressing himself directly to the young man rather than to the mediators:

I had come to put your people in your place. But now I feel only shame. Though I insulted your people, you still called me Father. It is you who speaks with wisdom, and me who has not seen the truth. What you have said is true. We who are chiefly have always looked down on you because you have no chief, but we have not understood the denigration you suffered. I beg you, my son, to forgive me.

At this point the younger Konkomba man stood, walked to the chief, then knelt and gripped his lower leg, a sign of deep respect. He vocalized a single and audible "Na-a," a word of affirmation and acceptance. While all was not resolved, a full-blown Ghanaian civil war was averted.[77]

Does the young Konkomba boy remind you of the Canaanite woman? Does the Dagomba chief remind you of Jesus in his response to the young boy?

For the sake of their daughters and sons, women of Liberia demonstrated great courage and tenacity in truth and in confronting the other. "Christian and Muslims united — form[ing] a thin but unshakable white line between the opposing forces, and successfully demanded an end to the fighting — armed only with white T-shirts and the courage of their convictions. In one remarkable scene, the women barricaded the site of stalled peace talks in Ghana and announced they would not move until a deal was done. Faced with eviction, they invoked the most powerful weapon in their arsenal — threatening to remove their clothes. It worked."[78]

It was a nonviolent, unconventional truth-telling and confrontation that finally led to peaceful transformation in Liberia in 2003 and is retold in the film *Pray the Devil Back to Hell.*[79]

Confronting the "other" often involves engaging the powers or complex systems of harm and oppression. In Liberia, truth-telling was unconventional, and confrontation involved a strong interfaith, nonviolent network of women. How and when do we find the courage and power to confront the "other" that is also an abusive or oppressive system? One inspiring journey unfolds in Somaly Mam's memoir *The Road of Lost Innocence.* Somaly Mam was born in a Cambodian village where her family experienced marginalization and abject poverty. She was sold into sexual slavery at the age of 12 by someone posing as her grandfather. The book chronicles unfathomable trauma, brutality and harm during the 10 years that she was moved from brothel to brothel in the sex trade of Southeast Asia. Having managed to escape, become married and begin a new life, Somaly tells about her encounter with the owner of a small house in her job as a real estate agent. The owner of this house was an elder who survived the trauma of an oppressive regime in their own country as well as noble yet largely unsuccessful attempts to change the unjust system. From him she received the wisdom that "the only thing to hope for is the peace you need to look after your own garden."[80] Reflecting on his words, she says, "I don't feel like I can change the world . . . I don't even try. I only want to change this small life that I see standing in front of me [that] is suffering. I want to change this small real thing that is the destiny of one little girl. And, then another, and another, because if I didn't, I wouldn't be able to live with myself or sleep at night."[81]

With one act following another and support from others who joined the journey, Somaly Mam went on to fight sex trafficking with fierce tenacity and courage. The Somaly Mam Foundation is a force around the globe in the fight against sexual slavery. It gives voice, shelter, liberation and recovery to victims of human trafficking; prepares survivors to create sustainable, meaningful lives; and provides advocacy to end this immoral and illegal trade.

Even though the girls and young women survivors affiliated with the

Somaly Mam Foundation may not directly engage their abusers, they are effectively confronting this abusive system of crime with their truth-telling, their story and their reintegration into free and sustainable lives. Their restorative journey places a humanizing face on this utterly dehumanizing system. The power of truth-telling and confrontation is that in setting free our stories of harm and recovery, others may also be humanized and find healing. This may not always include a direct encounter with an offender but does engage the powers and principalities of systems as we seek to break cycles of violence. Restorative practices beget restorative practices. Early in this study we acknowledged that journeys of reconciliation occur across a spectrum and are seldom neat and tidy. Our journeys must take into account the complex cycles of harm, woundedness and trauma. Part of the complexity is that the same dehumanizing cycles of violence hold the offender captive as well.

NAMING THE HARM AND GIVING BREAD
One of the most powerful stories we know of truth-telling and confronting the other is the story of Jesus' statements and actions at the Last Supper. Here he names the harm, but not to give a stone or retribution but to give bread.

After they have taken their places and are eating, what are the first words that we hear Jesus say? He says, "Truly I tell you, one of you will betray me, one who is eating with me." He adds, "It is one of the twelve, one who is dipping bread into the bowl with me" (Mark 14:17-20). Isn't this startling? What a way to start a dinner party! At his final dinner with his disciples, the first words of Jesus name the conflict that is the elephant in the room. Judas is going to betray Jesus. We see in John's Gospel the other way that Jesus names the conflict in which he found himself, the conflict written deep into the whole social fabric of his day. He moves from the head of the table to the foot of the table, takes the place of the least and washes the feet of all the disciples (John 13:3-17). In doing so, he names the structural and systemic problem of his society. He turns the society upside down.

There is nothing sentimental or individualistic or pietistic about this meal. The meal is not privatized or spiritualized. There is nothing here that is romantic or escapist. At this Table we experience the real world, with real and deep conflict. Jesus sits at his last supper, under the shadow of the cross with the man who would betray him and 11 others who will desert him. Does that experience sound conflicted to you? And Jesus named it. Here we see the importance of "Naming" on the journey to reconciliation, as seen on Olga Botcharova's diagram in Chapter 4. Justice requires the naming. Truth requires the naming. Transformation requires the naming. What is un-named lies just beneath the surface. It often develops dis-ease. It gets worse until it explodes in very destructive ways. You must name it to heal it. Di-agnosis is necessary for treatment. The naming, for Jesus, was the only way to begin the process of transforming this conflict into something construc-tive, into a new covenant, into a new revelation. The naming also helps us to understand the significance of the bread and wine. In the naming, we begin to see our need. We experience our hunger. We feel our thirst. We know we need God and one another. We need to be reconciled and to be a reconciler.

REFRAMING

What Jesus does next is remarkable, radical and transforming in the context of his day and ours. After naming the conflict, he turns and offers everyone — Judas, Peter, everyone — bread and wine. Think about this gesture. He reaches over to Judas and gives him a portion of a loaf he has blessed, not cursed, and says to Judas, "Take; this is my body." He also gives this bread to Peter and all of the others who would deny him. Then he takes a cup, and after giving thanks, he gives it to them, and all of them drink from it — *all* means Judas and Peter. He says, "This is my blood of the covenant, which is poured out for many" (Mark 14:22-24). The bread is the symbol of God's sustenance of God's creation best symbolized by the manna in the wilderness. The wine is a sign of the heavenly banquet (see 1 Corinthians 11:23-26 and Matthew 26:26-29). It is a sign of the new covenant between God and God's people, a covenant of forgiveness and reconciliation. The one cup symbolizes the unity of the body in Christ gathered at the table. Jesus names the conflict, but not in order to give a stone or to set the stage for retribution and punishment. He names it and then gives bread and wine. Indeed, he gives his life.

Here Jesus reframes our whole reality and the way we are to respond to conflict, differences and harm. This is a different reality than the temptation in the wilderness where "the tempter came and said to him, 'If you are the Son of God, command these stones to become loaves of bread'" (Matthew 4:3). This reframing is a different reality from the world of Judas and the reality of our world, a different way to deal with betrayal and harm. This reframing is a different way of dealing with violence, where you name the harm and give bread to your enemy. You name the conflict and respond with the gift of forgiveness. Think of what he has done with bread and wine, whose ingredients have gone through a process of being beaten, ground and trodden underfoot. This act of giving bread and wine is the symbolic act of forgiveness written deep in the Last Supper.

The frame within which Jesus calls us to live out our lives is not the frame of naming to punish but the frame of naming to give bread. Here we move from blaming to naming, from punishment to accountability, from retribution to forgiveness. The naming becomes a different reality in the context of the gift of bread and forgiveness. When the second step in the process after naming is giving bread, the tone of the naming is changed. It does not have the tone of blaming or humiliation. It does not have the "feel" of a statement to punish or wound or humiliate or dismiss. It creates a difference in the speaker and in the hearer. It opens up a different spirit in the speaker. It opens up in the hearer, in large part because of this different spirit, the possibility of openness to real accountability as opposed to a purely defensive response. There is a judgment here, but it is the judgment of love.

Remembering Jesus' Last Supper as we participate in the ritual of Holy Communion, we see the Table as a place where we receive the gift of communal as well as personal forgiveness. We are also called to forgive, which we will explore in our own Chapter 7. We see the Table as the place where we receive the word of reconciliation but also where we are spiritually formed into reconcilers, empowered to name and give bread, empowered to practice reconciliation.

We are reminded of a story from the South African Truth and Reconciliation Commission. In the days of apartheid, seven youth were killed by the South African military in an ambush. One of the men who participated in executing the youth testified before the commission. In the room were the mothers of these young men. After he finished testifying, the mothers were asked if they wanted to say anything. The spokeswoman for the group of mothers said that they did want to speak. She turned to the young man and said, "You are going to listen to our anger. Sit there and listen." One after another, these mothers spoke of the pain they had suffered. Then, after all had finished talking, one of the mothers turned to the man, who was totally crushed, and said, "Come here. Come here; let me hold you. Let me forgive you. I have no son, now. But I want you to be my son, so that you will never do these things again." She named the conflict. She then offered bread — indeed, her life.

Exercise

In light of several of the stories that have been read and discussed, the leader invites the group to think about their own journeys and the journeys of those they know are in need of healing.

- Provide a white T-shirt and or a piece of paper along with fabric paint or markers for each participant.
- Persons may join with another person with whom they are comfortable.
- Invite each person to prayerfully consider the truth or harm that they feel led to name.
- The naming of the truth or harm might be related to a person, a system or both. How will this be given voice? How does this expand your understanding of the church's mission as it is led to address this truth or this harm?
- Invite each person to record her or his thoughts on the paper or make a witness on the T-shirt.

- After about 15 minutes, come back to the Circle and ask each person to share as he or she is able to.

Concluding Ritual

The leader begins a closing blessing by saying the following to the group: "As bread for our journey, I offer this good word [name a word for the journey]." Continue clockwise, left to right around the Circle until everyone has offered a word of sustenance to the group. The leader closes by saying, "Let us give thanks for this bread." Persons may share refreshments and pieces of bread as they close.

Notes

74. See Robert Allen Warrior, "A Native American Perspective: Canaanites, Cowboys, and Indians," and Renita J. Weems, "Re-Reading for Liberation: African American Women and the Bible," *Voices from the Margin*, ed. R.S. Sugirtharajah (New York: Orbis Books, 2006), pp. 235-241, 27-38.

75. See also Appendix B for more about truth-telling and truth commissions.

76. Henry Wadsworth Longfellow, quoted in *The Chautauquan*, Vol. 4 (October 1883–July 1884), p. 211.

77. John Paul Lederach, op. cit., *The Moral Imagination*, pp. 7-9.

78. Weiman Seid and Jenny Lawhorn of Fat Dot, New York Press/Publicity: www.praythedevilbacktohell.com.

79. The film was released in 2008 by Fork Films and Wide Angle Productions.

80. Somaly Mam, *The Road of Lost Innocence* (New York: Spiegel and Grau, 2008), p. 128.

81. Ibid, p. 129.

Chapter 6

rehumanizing the other and the choice to forgive
the story of the prodigal

"But we had to celebrate and rejoice, because this brother of yours was dead and has come to life; he was lost and has been found."

—Luke 15:32

Preparation

- Read Luke 15:11-32.
- In your journal write all of the questions you have about this text as well as your own reflections.
- Spend some time with your questions, letting these questions go deeper and deeper. Note your insights.
- Look at the questions we have asked and write down your thoughts as to where these questions lead you, which may include other questions.
- Spend some time with the text and your journaling before you turn to the reflections that follow.
- After you have read the Reflection section, write down in your journal other insights and questions you have.

Setup

A small round table is in the middle of the room with a circle of chairs around the table. On the table is a single candle and anointing oil or balm. It is also set as if the group were going to have a "feast" with linens and food, either light refreshments or samples of food for a meal following the study, with each participant bringing an item of food or favorite dish to share. Consider using the small book *Three Simple Rules* by Bishop Rueben Job[82] as a talking piece. It is a reflection on the Wesleyan general rules: Do no harm. Do good. Stay in love with God.

Centering

The leader welcomes everyone as the candle is lighted.

Responsive Reading

Leader: Fire up the cooking pots!

Set a new place at the table . . .

Just in case she (he) comes home.[83]

ALL: I tell you, there is joy in the presence of the angels of God over one sinner who repents (Luke 15:10b).

— Safiyah Fosua

The Africana Worship Book: Year C, © 2008 by Discipleship Resources. Used by permission.

Prayers

The leader invites those gathered to a time of quiet reflection, thinking about the experience of forgiveness in their lives. After a few minutes, the leader invites persons to join in praying the "The Lord's Prayer."
(See, for example, **UMH #894, #895**)

Hymn

"Help Us Accept Each Other"　　(UMH #560)
or "Amazing Grace"　　(UMH #378)

Relational Covenant

The leader reminds everyone of the relational covenant that is posted on the wall. The covenant is read, and everyone affirms his or her commitment to the covenant.

Reading of the Text

The leader invites participants to read in three groups. Simply ask the first few persons to your left to be Group 1, the next few persons in the Circle to be Group 2 and the next few persons to be Group 3. Participants are invited to read the text in the following way.

Group 1

Then Jesus said, "There was a man who had two sons. The younger of them said to his father, 'Father, give me the share of the property that will belong to me.' So he divided his property between them."

Group 2

A few days later the younger son gathered all he had and traveled to a distant country, and there he squandered his property in dissolute living. When he had spent everything, a severe famine took place throughout that country, and he began to be in need.

Group 3

So he went and hired himself out to one of the citizens of that country, who sent him to his fields to feed the pigs. He would gladly have filled himself with the pods that the pigs were eating, and no one gave him anything.

Group 1

But when he came to himself he said, "How many of my father's hired hands have bread enough and to spare, but here I am dying of hunger! I will get up and go to my father, and I will say to him, 'Father, I have sinned against heaven and before you; I am no longer worthy to be called your son; treat me like one of your hired hands.'"

Group 2

So he set off and went to his father. But while he was still far off, his father saw him and was filled with compassion; he ran and put his arms around him and kissed him. Then the son said to him, "Father, I have sinned against heaven and before you; I am no longer worthy to be called your son."

Group 3

But the father said to his slaves, "Quickly, bring out a robe — the best one — and put it on him; put a ring on his finger and sandals on his feet. And get the fatted calf and kill it, and let us eat and celebrate, for this son of mine was dead and is alive again; he was lost and is found!" And they began to celebrate.

Group 1

Now his elder son was in the field, and when he came and approached the house, he heard music and dancing. He called one of the slaves and asked what was going on. He replied, "Your brother has come, and your father has killed the fatted calf, because he has got him back safe and sound."

Group 2

Then he became angry and refused to go in. His father came out and began to plead with him. But he answered his father, "Listen! For all these years I have been working like a slave for you, and I have never disobeyed your command, yet you have never given me even a young goat so that I might celebrate with my friends. But when this son of yours came back, who has devoured your property with prostitutes, you killed the fatted calf for him!"

Group 3

Then the father said to him, "Son, you are always with me, and all that is mine is yours. But we had to celebrate and rejoice, because this brother of yours was dead and has come to life; he was lost and has been found."

Questions

Leader: What follows are just some suggested questions to help you formulate questions for group discussion. We would suggest having four or five questions prepared. Others will flow from the conversation. After each question you ask, use the talking piece passed around the Circle to the left, to hear all of the voices as participants respond to the question. Then hold the talking piece so that the conversation can flow naturally, building on what has been said. When you get to the second question, follow the same practice with the talking piece.

- As you think about the Prodigal, the brother and the father, with which aspects of each do you identify?
- What does it mean to you that the Prodigal "came to himself?" Have you had an experience like this? Have you experienced practicing what you would say when you prepared to meet someone from who you are or were estranged?
- How have you experienced apologizing and trying to make things right?
- What do you learn from the parable about forgiveness and reconciliation?
- Imagine sitting in circle or at table with the two sons together. What would you say to them? What do you think they might say to each other as they truly engaged each other?

 REHUMANIZING THE OTHER AND THE CHOICE TO FORGIVE

These reflections are to stimulate your own thinking, not to limit the possible interpretations and the finding of what is meaningful to you in the passages.

THE SETTING AND STORY OF THE PRODIGAL, THE BROTHER AND THE FATHER

"There was a man who had two sons." Amy-Jill Levine tells us that this phrase, a familiar storytelling introduction for first century Jews at the time of Jesus, would have immediately informed the readers that these two would not get along and that there would be little "harmony" in the family.[84] This particular story is among the many teachings of Jesus on discipleship along his journey to Jerusalem (Luke 9:51-19:27). Jesus often challenges the religious leaders in these teachings, and contemporary eyes might see an anti-Jewish polemic. As we mentioned in our reflections on the other gospels, generalizing this tone is not helpful. What is important is the sharpness of Jesus' teaching that hits at the heart of ancient teachings and customs that we see in the life of the older brother and invites us to think more deeply about the importance of relationships.

The younger son and the father

The parable begins with a question about a custom of that day — inheritance — and the surprising request by the younger son for his portion of the inheritance. Equally surprising is the response of the father in honoring his request. The son then leaves the relationship with his family and travels to a "distant country" (Luke 15:13). There he "squandered his property in dissolute living" — hence the term "prodigal," to give or throw away with reckless abandonment (15:13). The younger son is down and out and hungry. He is willing to eat with the pigs, he's so hungry. No one gives him any help. Focused on his hunger he imagines the abundance in his father's household, where even the hired hands have full bellies. He is desperate, "I'm dying of hunger!" That is when something happens — when the body and spirit are yearning for change. We are told "he came to himself" (15:17). He was lost, he was lost from himself. He came to see that he was lost from the relational web of his family. He says twice in this story, "I am no longer worthy to be called your son" (15:19, 21). He does not see how he can recover the relationship he had with his father, with his family.

So, just like Jacob in the Genesis journey of reconciliation, the younger son decides to prepare for an encounter. This is what I will do: I'll tell him how wrong I've been and that I've sinned against him and God. I'll tell him I don't even deserve to be treated as well as your hired hands — referencing a social order in the household of that day. He is trying in his own way to apologize and be accountable for his actions.

"But while he was still far off" his father saw him. The father, unlike the son, never let go of the relationship. He watched. He waited. He ran to embrace his son. It is interesting that the compassionate father embraces the son before the son can confess and apologize. A confession then follows: "Father, I have sinned against heaven and you, I am no longer worthy to be called your son" (15:21). But the father immediately calls for a great party! Bring out the best clothes, fire up the pot, ". . . let us eat and celebrate for this son of mine was dead and is alive, was lost and is found!"

In this chapter, we've just heard the parable of the lost sheep, which we discuss in our own Chapter 3, and the lost coin (Luke 15:1-10). Now we have the lost son who is found and has come home. The grief of the loss of this child is turned to joy. Like the embrace with Jacob and Esau, forgiveness is a gift. The gift of the homecoming of the younger son is a gift of restored relationship to his father.

The elder son and the father

The oldest brother may be called the "dutiful" one. He's done his part. He never strayed from the flock and he is angry. He's not about to join this lavish and ridiculous party. It is not just! His father pleads with him to come. The elder son laments that he has not received such lavishness. And the father reminds the elder, "Son, you are always with me, and all that is mine is yours." Here we learn that the Prodigal has been embraced, restored to the family, but not restored to his inheritance. There is justice, but it is not retributive.

The elder son has everything he was given from the beginning of the story — his property, his place in the household, his relationship with his father. This is a household of abundance — all are fed well! And now, he has his brother who was thought to be lost if not dead. His brother is alive and in his midst.

We understand the response of the older brother. Isn't it unjust and against the rules to honor one who squanders his inheritance more than the one who works hard, to honor one who breaks with the family more than the one who is faithful? Miroslav Volf, in *Exclusion and Embrace*, says,

> The older brother employs *moral categories* and constructs his brother's departure along the axis of "bad or good" behavior: the brother has "devoured your property with prostitutes" (v. 30). The father, though keenly aware of the moral import of his younger son's behavior, employs *relational categories* and constructs his son's departure along the axis of "lost/found" and "alive (to him)/dead (to him)." Relationship is prior to moral rules; moral performance may do *something* to the relationship, but relationship is not *grounded* in moral performance. Hence the *will* to embrace is independent of the quality of behavior, though at the same time "repentance," "confession," and the "consequences of one's actions" all have their own proper place.[85]

The younger son and the elder son

What about the relationship of the two sons? Will they see each other as brothers again? Will the elder brother be able to journey through his anger to embrace compassion and see the gift of his brother's return? Would he be able to stomach this brother who, for him, had been too close in contact with sinners and swine? This would likely be a hard thing for one who was formed and nurtured in a tradition of purity that was hostile to those "outsiders." What about the younger son, will he be able to approach his brother with the same sense of contrition and openness with which he approached his father? Will he also be able to have compassion for his brother and his experience? Will the two be able to sit at the table together? Will the three be able to sit together? Will they be able to negotiate a just and reconciled relationship, the final stage in Olga Botcharova's journey to reconciliation?

The Journey of Forgiveness, Rehumanizing the Other and the Choice to Forgive

In Chapters 4 and 5 we touched on important guideposts of the journey of forgiveness and reconciliation following harm or trauma — finding safety, mourning loss, confronting fears, and naming or telling one's truth and one's story. Now we look more closely at the importance of the other's story, the one who has harmed, and the power of rehumanizing the other and the gift of forgiveness.

Recognizing the other's story is at the heart of rehumanizing the one who harmed you and to moving toward a decision to forgive, as noted in Olga Botcharova's diagram in Chapter 4. Carolyn Yoder says, "The universal cry, 'Why me?' or 'Why us?' reflects the longing to find reason and meaning in difficult life events. Yet continually asking these often unanswerable questions keeps us stuck. Together with suppressed fears, these questions provoke the greatest anger at everything and everyone associated with the perpetrator. To restore the ability to think rationally, the question needs to be reframed to 'Why them: Why did they do it, and why did they do it to us?' This reframing opens the way to search for root causes and to acknowledge that the other, the enemy, also has a story."[86]

This reframing is not about condoning what happened, but it does offer a way forward. Life is always more complex than individual narratives. The "enemies" are fellow human beings, children of God. In the story of the person who harmed us we find the lessons of interconnections and interdependence. We develop an understanding that allows us to act rationally. It can even yield compassion.

The lives of Jo Berry and Patrick Magee were brought together by the Brighton hotel bombing of the Tory Conference in 1984 in Brighton, England. Patrick Magee, an activist with the Irish Republican Army (IRA), was given multiple life sentences for the bombing. Jo Berry's father, Sir Anthony Berry MP, was killed in the bombing. The ongoing conflict and struggle for peace in Northern Ireland was punctuated by acts of violence and multiple attempts to wage peace throughout most of the 20th century. The 1999 "Good Friday Agreement" marked a significant step toward peace. One aspect of the agreement included the release of Patrick Magee and other activists who had been incarcerated. For Jo and Patrick, we witness the reframing and rehumanizing of the one who has harmed. In Jo's words:

> I wanted to meet Pat to put a face to the enemy, and see him as a real human being. At our first meeting I was terrified, but I wanted to acknowledge the courage it had taken him to meet me. We talked with an extraordinary intensity. I shared a lot about my father, while Pat told me some of his story. Over the past two and a half years of getting to know Pat, I feel I've been recovering some of the humanity I lost when that bomb went off. Pat is also on a journey to recover his humanity. I know that he sometimes finds it hard to live with the knowledge that he cares for the daughter of someone he killed through his terrorist actions. Perhaps more than anything I've realised that no matter which side of the conflict you're on, had we all lived each other's lives, we could all have done what the other did."[87]

Jo and Pat now work together in efforts to curb violence and work for peace through the organization, Building Bridges for Peace.[88]

In the experience of the Amish community's response to the West Nickel Mines School shooting we find more learnings about the power of rehumanizing the other and the gift of forgiveness. The school shooting in Nickel Mines, Pennsylvania, attracted widespread media and public attention in October 2006. On a clear, warm autumn day, a gunman known to his victims killed five children and critically wounded five others before ending his own life in a devastating shooting rampage in a small Amish[89] school. The story soon became front and center in many North American media centers. Certainly some were surprised to read and hear such a headline about a relatively isolated Amish community. The focus of the media and the general public's attention, however, were the swift and seemingly uncoordinated acts of forgiveness on the part of the families and community members of the Old Order Amish.

Late into the night after the fifth girl died in her mother's arms, the grandfather emerged from the hospital to face the lights of the media and participated in this exchange:

> "Do you have any anger toward the gunman's family?" [the reporter] asked.
>
> "No."
>
> "Have you already forgiven them?"
>
> "In my heart, yes."
>
> "How is that possible?"
>
> "Through God's help."[90]

This was just one of many stories of grace that began to flow from the Pennsylvania community in the face of this trauma and harm. Family members of Amish victims visited soon afterward with family members of the gunman, recognizing that they were also victims. Money flowed into the community "from outside" as the media coverage raised awareness of the tragic events and the response. In addition to a fund for the Amish victims, the Amish offered money to the widow of the gunman and her children, setting up a fund for them as well.

The Amish typically would reject outside assistance according to their custom and practice. "The whole nation is grieving," said one Amish leader. "By letting them give, it helps them, too." The [Accountability] Committee therefore agreed to accept outside donations so that others wouldn't be deprived "of the blessing of giving."[91]

In rare public exchanges with the media, Amish leaders spoke of the comfort received from each act of kindness and even confessed that their "perceptions of 'worldly' and 'outsiders' [had] been challenged." They were heartened by the response.

The ongoing journey continued with the families of those killed, and the family of the gunman. Most of the Amish funerals were private; however, when the family of the gunman gathered to bury him in the cemetery of Georgetown United Methodist Church, more than half of those present were Amish.[92]

Continuing the journey of grieving, storying, rehumanizing and restorying, the families of the gunman and the children killed and wounded gathered in a local fire hall several weeks after the shooting. "We went around the circle and introduced ourselves," an Amish leader said. "Amy [the gunman's wife] just cried and cried and cried. We talked and cried and talked and cried. . . . There were a lot of tears shed that day. There was a higher power in the room."[93] The power of these expressions of forgiveness gave great freedom to the family members of the offender, releasing them from a heavy burden, releasing them from being defensive and opening up their story.

The sharing of stories eventually revealed deep tragic pain that the gunman had wrestled with following the death of his baby daughter several years before the shooting. Witnesses even tell stories that he apologized to the young girls and to his wife prior to his act of violence.

"Why is everybody so surprised?" asked one Amish man about his community's response to the attack. "It's just standard forgiveness, it's what everybody should be doing." The practice is a way of life embedded in the community and centered on Matthew 6:12. "Help us forgive others as Jesus forgives us."[94]

There is much within the Amish community about which those "outside" are critical as well. No community lives in perfection. The journey of forgiveness and reconciliation is never perfect. Living up to the world's expectations of forgiveness is a new element for this community.

A key learning is that "Amish believe that gracious actions extended to the offender are an important aspect of authentic forgiveness."[95] It is still a journey, and it is a willed act that lives in hope of reconciliation.

Walter Everett was the pastor of the First United Methodist Church in

Hartford, Connecticut. One night he learned that his son had been killed by another resident of his son's apartment house. He experienced all of the emotions that one would expect, including deep anger and bitterness. He started going to a meeting of a group of people who had also experienced the death of a loved one through a criminal act. As he attended these meetings he discovered there were people in the group who had been coming for years, up to 30 years, and they were as angry and bitter as ever. They were tragically impacted by the crime and now they were dying within themselves. He decided this was not the way his son would want him to live or he wanted to live. He realized this anger was only hurting him and that he needed to be free of the thrall of the offense. Over time he reached out to the young man who killed his son. In the process, he came to forgive the young man. Later, he officiated at the young man's wedding. Together they now speak to groups about forgiveness and restorative justice.

Walter invited Tom to address the first international meeting of Murder Victims' Families for Reconciliation. There we listened to the stories, stories very similar to Walter's. I (Tom) also looked into the eyes of these mothers and fathers, brothers and sisters, daughters and sons. I saw the pain, but I also saw a joy and peace that I did not expect. In their journey toward forgiveness and reconciliation, they had reached deep places, to the heart of God.

As Walter Everett discovered, not undertaking the journey to forgiveness involves a double injury — one imposed from the outside and the second imposed from the inside. We can get stuck in the anger and the bitterness. We do further harm to ourselves as seen in, for example, substance abuse, workaholism, overeating. We experience physical ailments and emotional ailments such as depression, apathy, anxiety and inability to trust. We also can do harm to those near us and to the one who harmed us and continue the cycles of woundedness, retribution and violence.

What about seemingly unforgivable acts — atrocities against humanity, the Rwanda genocide, the Holocaust, the raping of women and girls, profiting from impoverishment of peoples and resources? We must name these evils and oppose them. And what about the strong formation in many of our communities to have women forgive quickly? We must be honest and enter authentic and full journeys together. The very act of bearing witness to harm and trauma and atrocities as we studied in Chapter 5 is part of the journey toward reconciliation. We must bear witness and hear witness. We must continue to set the table and expect that when we are lost, there is the possibility of being found. As Desmond Tutu says, there is "no future without forgiveness."[96] In the spirit of *ubuntu* we are who we are because of our relationships. When I dehumanize you, I dehumanize myself. We exist in a web of interconnected relationships with one another and God's creation. If we, all of us, are in the heart of God, God's own creation, then how can we do otherwise?

Forgiveness is a journey with no single script. As Olga Botcharova notes in her schema (page 103), it is a choice. It is a choice that cannot be coerced or manipulated. Forgiveness is primarily a gift we give ourselves, as Walter Everett learned. It is a way we reassert our power and our dignity. It is also a gift we give the other, as seen in the story of the Amish. The capacity to offer and receive forgiveness is critical to breaking the cycles of woundedness, retribution and violence. Forgiveness is not reconciliation, but for Olga Botcharova and Bishop Tutu it is the only way to reconciliation.

In the next chapter we will explore the justice that is needed for reconciliation, the last elements on Olga Botcharova's diagram of the movement from aggression to reconciliation. In this chapter we see the connection between rehumanizing the other, the choice to forgive and reconciliation as seen in the actions of the father of the Prodigal.

Exercise

- The leader invites participants to gather in three groups. (You may wish to use the three reading groups.)
- Each group is provided healing balm or oil and a handkerchief.
- In a time of silence, each person is invited to reflect on the journey of forgiveness and a situation or person that yearns to forgive or be forgiven.

- After a few minutes, invite the small groups to pray with one another, anointing one another with oil or balm on the back of the hand or forehead.
- When anointing, say to one another, "Tender and compassionate God, Heal us." When all have been offered the balm or oil, move into the larger circle.

Concluding Ritual

The leader invites all to join the litany.

One: Out of the depths, we cry to you, Lord.

Many: Hear our voice. Hear our cry.

One: Listen

Many: Between each heartbeat.

One: Listen

Many: Between each breath.

One: Listen

Many: To things we don't say,

One: Can't say,

Many: Things from which we run away.

Silence

One: If you counted every wrong we've done, who could stand, Lord?

Many: But you forgive.

One: So we wait on you.

Many: Our souls wait.

One: In your word is hope.

Many: We long for you,

One: More than the endless night looks for dawn,

Many: More than hunger looks for food,

One: We hope.

Many: For God is our hope and our salvation.

— Kwasi Kena

The leader then invites persons to share signs of peace and reconciliation with one another. If a meal is shared, all move to the place of the feast.

Notes

82. Rueben Job, *Three Simple Rules* (Nashville: Abingdon Press), 2007. This book is a reflection on the General Rules in the Wesleyan tradition.

83. "21st Century Worship Resources," General Board of Discipleship, United Methodist Church.

84. Amy-Jill Levine, *The Misunderstood Jew* (San Francisco: Harper, 2006), p. 36.

85 Miroslav Volf, *Exclusion and Embrace, A Theological Exploration of Identity, Otherness and Reconciliation* (Nashville: Abingdon Press, 1996), p. 164.

86. Carolyn Yoder, *The Little Book of Trauma Healing* (Intercourse, Pa.: Good Books, 2005), p. 55.

87. The Forgiveness Project Registered Charity Number: 1103922 (www.theforgivenessproject.com). Used by permission.

88. See www.buildingbridgesforpeace.org. See also Appendix C.

89. The Amish are an Old Order band of Christians who choose to live by certain customs of simplicity and to live separately from many mainstream North American communities.

90. Donald B. Kraybill, Steven Nolt and Davis L. Weaver-Zercher, *Amish Grace: How Forgiveness Transcended Tragedy* (San Francisco: Jossey-Bass Wiley Press, 2007), p. 45.

91. Ibid, p. 33.

92. Ibid, p. 45.

93. Ibid, p. 46.

94. Ibid.

95. Ibid, p. xiii.

96. Desmond Mpilo Tutu, *No Future Without Forgiveness* (New York: Image, Doubleday, 1999), p. 31.

Chapter 7

repentance and restitution —making things right

the story of abigail and david and the story of zacchaeus

"Blessed be your good sense, and blessed be you, who have kept me today from bloodguilt and from avenging myself by my own hand! For as surely as the LORD the God of Israel lives, who has restrained me from hurting you, unless you had hurried and come to meet me, truly by morning there would not have been left to Nabal so much as one male." Then David received from her hand what she had brought him; he said to her, "Go up to your house in peace; see, I have heeded your voice, and I have granted your petition."

—1 Samuel 25:33-35

When Jesus came to the place, he looked up and said to him, "Zacchaeus, hurry and come down; for I must stay at your house today." So he hurried down and was happy to welcome him. All who saw it began to grumble and said, "He has gone to be the guest of one who is a sinner." Zacchaeus stood there and said to the Lord, "Look, half of my possessions, Lord, I will give to the poor; and if I have defrauded anyone of anything, I will pay back four times as much."

—Luke 19: 5-8

Preparation

- Read 1 Samuel 25:1-38 and Luke 19:1-10.
- In your journal write all of the questions you have about this text as well as your own reflections.
- Spend some time with your questions, letting these questions go deeper and deeper. Note your insights.
- Look at the questions we have asked and write down your thoughts as to where these questions lead you, which may include other questions.
- Spend some time with the text and your journaling before you turn to the reflections that follow.
- After you have read the Reflection section, write down in your journal other insights and questions you have.

Setup

A small round table is in the middle of the room with a circle of chairs around the table. On the table is a single candle. Some light refreshments are in the room. Consider using as a talking piece a small cloth bag of coins.

Centering

The leader welcomes everyone as the candle is lighted.

Opening Prayer (Unison)

God our Mother and Father, we come to you as children.
Be with us as we learn to see one another with new eyes,
Hear one another with new hearts,
And treat one another in a new way. Amen. (BOW#466)

Hymn

"Pues Si Vivimos" **(UMH #356)** ("When We Are Living")
or "What Does the Lord Require of You" **(TFWS #2174)**

The leader tests consensus about using a small cloth bag of coins as a talking piece.

Relational Covenant

The leader reminds everyone of the relational covenant that is posted on the wall. The covenant is read, and everyone affirms his or her commitment to the covenant.

Reading of the Text

A volunteer or volunteers read 1 Samuel 25:14-20, 23-25, 28-33. All will read together Luke 19:1-10.

Questions

Leader: What follows are just some suggested questions to help you formulate questions for group discussion. We would suggest having four or five questions prepared. Others will flow from the conversation. After each question you ask, use the talking piece passed around the Circle to the left, to hear all of the voices as participants respond to the question. Then hold the talking piece so that the conversation can flow naturally, building on what has been said. When you get to the second question, follow the same practice with the talking piece.

- How does Abigail "make things right" between her household and David? What is it that makes David change his mind?
- Zacchaeus is described as short in stature and even climbs the tree to see Jesus. Why do you think he was moved to see him?
- Why does the crowd seem so concerned (grumbling) about Jesus going to the house of Zacchaeus? Is Zacchaeus a changed man? What do you learn about repentance, restitution and personal accountability from this encounter?
- How in your experience have you tried to apologize for harm or wrongdoing and make things right?

REFLECTION — REPENTANCE AND RESTITUTION—MAKING THINGS RIGHT

These reflections are to stimulate your own thinking, not to limit the possible interpretations and the finding of what is meaningful to you in the passages.

THE NEED FOR ENGAGEMENT TO ADDRESS HARM AND PERSONAL ACCOUNTABILITY

In the book of 1 Samuel Chapter 25, we meet David after Samuel has died and he was spared by Saul. David had gone into the wilderness of Paran. When we meet him in this story, he has been keeping watch over the land, shepherds and sheep of a rich landowner in Carmel. When he learns that the rancher will be shearing three thousand sheep on a feast day, David seeks recompense for the services he has rendered. The landowner is Nabal, meaning "fool" or ill-behaved. He refuses to share with David and his men any food that he has set aside for his shearers, claiming he does not know him, although his shepherds tell him how David has protected them. Upon hearing that Nabal has rejected his request, David straps on his sword and swears retribution.

In this midst of this explosive conflict, Abigail, Nabal's wife, receives word from one of the young men of her household. The young man tells her how David and his men protected Nabal's shepherds and his sheep. He appeals to Abigail's discretion, warning about Nabal who is so "ill-natured" and the anger of David. The young man knew that Abigail had the ability to defuse this situation, a situation where "evil has been decided against our master and against all his house" (1 Samuel 25:17).

Loaded with plenty of food, Abigail secretly (not telling Nabal) makes her way to see David along with some of the young men. We are reminded of Jacob as he traveled with gifts to meet Esau. Abigail is prepared to engage David in a way that restores the relation that her husband has breached and saves her household from destruction.

We have been told that Abigail is beautiful and clever. When she sees

David, she falls before him and pleads that he not take seriously this ill-natured fellow Nabal but deal with her instead. She treats him with respect and calls him "Lord." Even referencing the sling, she reminds David of Goliath and his own vocation — being appointed "prince over Israel" (Samuel 25:30). She presents him with gifts that David should have received from Nabal saying, "And now let this present that your servant has brought to my lord be given to the young men who follow my lord" (Samuel 25:27). She then asks for forgiveness, "Please forgive the trespass of your servant" (Samuel 25:28). Does this remind you of the Canaanite woman as she addressed Jesus, or the young Konkomba as he addressed the chief of the Dagombas, whom we studied in our own Chapter 5?

David hears and responds, "Blessed be the Lord, the God of Israel, who sent you to meet me today! Blessed be your good sense, and blessed be you, who have kept me today from bloodguilt and from avenging myself by my own hand!" (Samuel 25:32-33). Without her intervention, "I would not have left Nabal so much as one male" (Samuel 25:34). Abigail's actions to address the harm experienced by David and to make things right with him broke the cycle of violence that David was ready to pursue. She saved him from bloodguilt, from what would have only led to cycles of violence. We see how David and his people and Abigail and her people are served by Abigail's actions.

Abigail returned to Nabal who was feasting like a king. In the morning after Abigail told him these things, he died. We're told "his heart died within him; he became like stone" (Samuel 25:37). Does this remind you of the response of Judas in taking his own life when he realized what he had done?

On the journey of reconciliation, there comes a time when one who has offended needs to engage the other and make things right. When her husband refused to do what was right, Abigail took responsibility and acted for the good of all. On behalf of those in harm's way, Abigail created an opportunity to remind David of his better self — who he was destined to be as a leader on behalf of God's people. This identity was contrasted with the self-indulgent and contemptuous nature of Nabal. This wise approach with David helps him see differently, to embrace beauty and life rather than death and destruction.

A JOURNEY TO REALLY SEE JESUS AND THE RESPONSE OF PERSONAL ACCOUNTABILITY

Jesus encounters Zacchaeus near the end of his journey to Jerusalem. There has been much teaching and storytelling and confrontation with religious leaders as the fullness of who Jesus really is continues to be revealed. Jesus encounters Zacchaeus near the end of his journey to Jerusalem. The journey for Zacchaeus to see Jesus comes directly after the healing of the blind man begging on the roadside. Jesus helps those who want to see. He also sees into the hearts of people, including Zacchaeus.

Zacchaeus was a tax collector, a Jewish official in the Roman government. As we've learned from the teachings of Jesus in Luke, tax collectors were viewed by the populace as corrupt and unjust. The "tax man" was considered a thief, and he most likely exploited those with little means for the sake of the rich and the powerful. The unwelcoming crowds were not going to make a way for this little man, whom they hated. What moves this government official to shatter rules of decorum and run ahead and climb a tree like a child to see Jesus? In this story, we see him leaning from a branch with excitement to get a closer look.

There! Jesus spotted him. Jesus told him to come down for he's going to stay at his house. Happy, he hurried down to welcome him. The crowd groaned, "He has gone to be the guest of one who was a sinner" (Luke 19:7). Zacchaeus seems to hear the despair and sets the record right immediately saying, "Look, half of my possessions, Lord, I will give to the poor, and if I have defrauded anyone of anything, I will pay back four times as much" (19:8). He not only wants to see and be seen; he wants to make things right. Jesus claims that Zacchaeus, a Jewish official in the Roman government, is also a "son of Abraham." Zacchaeus sees Jesus for who he really is, one who often breaks the rules of social order to bring about salvation. What a transformational experience!

The word "house" (*oikos*) could refer to our spiritual home. Jesus has residence there. It most likely also points to the "household" — the home, family, the community — and its entire well-being. "Protected and sustained by the household, the members assume responsibility to take care of the household for the good of all."[97] So, Jesus wants to stay at his house, and Zacchaeus deals with the very practical work of caring for the good of all. As one who has harmed others by taking more money than owed in taxes and benefiting from this corruption, he earnestly seeks a path of accountability. Jesus sees this as he spots Zacchaeus in the tree.

One has the sense that Zacchaeus has been listening to what Jesus has taught about riches, the eye of the needle, and little children. The one who called Levi a tax collector to follow him (Luke 5:32) has now called Zacchaeus to a new path. This "son of Abraham" has a conversion experience and remembers his own tradition of Jubilee[98] — restoring the debts in multiple. In seeing Jesus, he also sees more deeply into himself in the context of the life he has lived.

REPENTANCE AND RESTITUTION

These stories are stories of restorative justice. Abigail and Zacchaeus followed the journey of those who have harmed another — the journey that Jesus spelled out in Matthew 18, which we studied in our own Chapter 3. They each heard and understood the harm that had been done. They acknowledged the harm (confession) and then worked to make things right (repentance). This was the only way out of cycles of harm. According to Jesus in Matthew 18, this was the only way to enter the Kingdom of Heaven. According to Olga Botcharova's diagram found in Chapter 4, establishing justice is the last essential element on the journey to reconciliation.

The modern restorative justice movement is one of the most important movements of our time. It involves the rediscovery and the practice of what Jesus taught. The movement began in 1974 with two Mennonite probation officers in Canada. Two young men had vandalized 22 different homes. They were caught and brought before the court. Mark Yantzi and Dave

Worth asked the judge if they might try something different by having the two boys go to each person they had harmed, acknowledge their responsibility, listen to each describe how their acts had affected them and then work to repair the damage they had done. The judge finally supported this.

This example encouraged others, including a man named Howard Zehr,[99] who has been instrumental in the development of the modern movement. He began to develop a practice of engaging victims and offenders to hear the story of the harm that had been done and to encourage the offender to meet the needs of the victims through personal accountability. The movement has spread throughout the world, and different practices have emerged as people returned to their own practices of restorative justice that existed prior to the imposition of Western adversarial retributive systems.

One example of such a practice is the Family Group Conference (FGC), which grew out of traditional Maori practices in New Zealand. In 1989 the juvenile justice system of New Zealand was revolutionized so that the primary response to juvenile crime was the FGC with the court system as a backup. A key focus of the FGC is to get young offenders to take responsibility for and change their behavior. The participants in the process include family members, especially of the offender, other individuals significant to the parties and justice officials. The victims are first given the opportunity to tell their stories. At some point in the process, there is usually a family caucus where the family of the offender meets separately to work out a proposal for accountability to be brought back to the victim and the rest of the conference. The final plan must be a realistic plan of accountability that is accepted by all the participants. A modified version of this was developed by police in Australia.

What follows is an example of the dynamics of such a conference. In New Zealand, a conference was called to work with a young man who broke into a car, vandalized it and took some items that were important to the owners. The victims talked about how they had been harmed. The young offender, surrounded by his family, listened. His grandfather then stood up and told the young man how he had shamed the family and the community and that he needed to make restitution to the victims, with his uncle Joe giving him a job so he could earn the money. He also needed to make things right with his family and the community.

After he finished, the grandfather told his grandson that he still loved him, embraced him and told him that he would work with him to make things right. The Maori priest also talked about how the offender was going to work in the temple. The victims were vindicated and received restitution. In fact, they came away forgiving the young man who apologized in his own way but made it real by agreeing to do restitution. The offender accepted his accountability. There was a sense of healing as everyone left the room.

In the late 1990s the two of us (Stephanie and Tom) began to work together in responding to complaints filed against clergy. We began to reflect on the principles of restorative justice that had been adopted by the United Methodist Church in its Social Principles.[100] We believed that these same principles should be applied to our complaint processes. We developed what we called circles of accountability and healing. We brought together the complainants and the respondents and others to tell their stories and to work together to hear the needs of those harmed, to discover what the respondents could do to make things right and to work toward healing for all of the parties involved.

For example, in a case involving theft of money by a pastor, we brought together representatives from the church that had experienced the loss of money and trust, representatives of the bishop's cabinet and the board of ordained ministry who had experienced the breach of the covenant of ministry, the pastor, the pastor's wife, her best friend, his best friend and an ex-offender who could help us understand what the journey might be like for the pastor. We used a circle process like what you are using for this Bible Study. The circle first tried to understand the harm created by the theft by listening to the victims. We then all worked, including the pastor and the pastor's wife, to find a plan of accountability. All this was done by consensus. The process took place only if everyone agreed to participate. Remarkable results occurred.

We spent time prayerfully considering whether such a process could be used in cases of sexual abuse or misconduct. We knew that just a session with the victim and the offender carried with it an imbalance of power and the risks of revictimization. With the larger circle of support for each party and wise people present to help with the hearing and the decision making, and with much preparation, we found that we could provide reasonable safety and do healing work.

All of our circles begin and end with a ritual that is sensitive to the participants and where we recognize that we are in a sacred space. We always develop a relational covenant.

Since 2004, the complaint processes of the United Methodist Church have just resolution provisions that include principles of restorative justice: addressing harm through acceptance of personal responsibility.[101]

The aim of restorative justice is to identify the needs of the person harmed and to determine the obligations of the offender — and even the community — in addressing these harms. Instead of a punishment system, restorative justice creates an accountability system. What does the offender need to do personally to address the needs of the person harmed, to make things right? We are talking about real accountability to the victim. In the retributive system, third parties determine the punishment. This is coerced accountability, and, in our experience, the third-party punishment does not lead, in most cases, to acceptance of responsibility and to actions on the part of the offender personally to address the harms created. Punishment is often counterproductive to such accountability as it discourages empathy and encourages denial of responsibility. Most people in prison see themselves as victims, and in many ways they are. In fact, their crimes often come out of their own victimhood. The punishment system adds to this sense of victimhood. Restorative justice is able to see the offender in context but, more importantly, gives the offender the chance to take personal responsibility.

The stories of Abigail and Zacchaeus are remarkable stories of this personal accountability, of repentance and restitution. We see how the journey of restorative justice can lead to reconciliation.

REPENTANCE, RESTITUTION AND THE MINISTRY OF RECONCILIATION
Early in the study in Chapter 2 we explored Love of God, Neighbor and Self — the Great Commandment. We were reminded that we are relational by nature. Creation is relational and God is a relational being. At the heart of restorative justice is this understanding of relationship and the importance of the engagement of the other in community. To experience healing and restorative justice, we as Christians are called to engage harm, even that which is inextricably woven into the fabric of our communities and histories.

Megan McKenna relays the wisdom shared by an elder when a group had gone to visit the Acoma Pueblo, on a high mesa outside of Albuquerque. The visit was shortly after the events of 9/11.[102] After some laughter and engaging conversation, the group became intent on listening as the elder grew silent. "I'm sorry. I apologize. It was our fault. It was all our fault." No one knew what the man meant, or how to respond. He realized that they did not understand him, so he said again, "I'm so very sorry. We all are. It was — it is our fault. You see, we believe that we are all one. We have a saying that is sometimes translated as 'all our relations' — it means that we are all one — everything and everyone created: birds, fish, animals, four-leggeds, two-leggeds, all human beings everywhere in the world. And we are responsible for each other and what others do. So it is our fault. We have not lived as we should. If we were living as human beings, other human beings would not be driven to do such terrible things. They would not be without hope, and filled with so much despair. We are so sorry, please forgive us." His words left everyone in the group speechless, and they wandered off awkwardly. McKenna says when she heard this story it made perfect sense. "We must honor all our relations so that something as horrible as 9/11 can never happen again."[103]

Isn't this what we are commanded to do in loving God, neighbor and self? Jesus came to bring peace and called us to do the same. Paul recognizes that our calling in this deeply broken world is to a ministry of reconciliation, to be ambassadors of reconciliation (2 Corinthians 5:16-20). We know this involves grieving and confronting our fears, telling our stories to one another as we name in order to give bread, engaging one another so we can see the child of God in the other, rehumanizing the other. We know that there is no future without forgiveness. We know there is no future without taking personal responsibility and accountability for the harm we do. We know that there is no script for this journey of reconciliation, but it is the journey for which we were created and to which we are called.

Exercise
The leader invites persons to reflect on the prayer below silently and to join in the unison prayer.

"A Prayer for the Will to Repent" (in Unison) [104]
Lord, help me turn away from evil
Before it is too late
Before the children get the wrong idea
Before I ruin my health
Before I lose my job
Before I break my spouse's heart
Before I go to jail
Help me to turn away
Before the natural consequences of evil
Cannot be held back.
Before this mark on
An already-seared conscience
Becomes indelible.
Forgiving God, Loving God,
God-who-makes-a-way-out-of-no-way God
Help me to stop and turn away
Before it is too late!
Amen.

— Safiyah Fosua

- Providing paper and something to write with, find a place for quiet reflection in the room.
- Think about your journey of repentance and restitution.
- Choose one situation or concern and write your thoughts on how to acknowledge harm and make things right. The letters are for you personally.
- After 15 minutes, return to the Circle for reflection together.

Concluding Ritual

- Persons are invited to stand as they are able.
- The leader turns to the person to the left and says, "Take courage. In the name of Jesus Christ, you are already forgiven."
- That person then turns to the left and says, "Take courage. In the name of Jesus Christ, you are already forgiven."
- Continue around the Circle until everyone has received the word.

Gathering in the Circle again, the leader invites persons to pray together the Lord's Prayer as found in the UMH #896, using "debts" and "debtors."

All are invited to share signs of peace and reconciliation.

Notes

97. Gosbert T. M. Byamungu, "Grace as a Subversive Surprise: A Reading of Psalm 130 and Luke 19:1-10," *The Ecumenical Review*, Vol. 56, no. 3 (July 2004), p. 334.

98. Ivoni Richter Reime, "The Forgiveness of Debts in Matthew and Luke: For an Economy without Exclusion," in *Voices From the Margin*, ed. R.S. Sugirtharajah (New York: Orbis Books, 2006), p. 155.

99. See Appendix D.

100. Criminal and Restorative Justice, in "Social Principles," *The 2008 Book of Discipline of The United Methodist Church* (Nashville: The United Methodist Publishing House, 2008), Paragraph 164H, p. 126.

101. *The 2008 Book of Discipline of The United Methodist Church* (Nashville: The United Methodist Publishing House, 2008), paragraphs 361.1 and 2701.

102. The term 9/11 refers to the events of September 11, 2001, when four U.S. jetliners were hijacked by persons affiliated with al-Qaida terrorist cells. Two airplanes were flown into the twin World Trade Center towers in New York, New York. One was flown into the Pentagon building in Arlington, Virginia (Washington, D.C.), and another crashed in Shanksville, Pennsylvania. Nearly 3,000 persons from an estimated 70 nations lost their lives in the tragic events of that day (9/11).

103. Megan McKenna, *Matthew: The Book of Mercy* (New York: New City Press, 2007), pp. 117-118.

104. "21st Century Worship," General Board of Discipleship.

interfaith reconciliation

Chapter 8

reconciliation of the jews and the gentiles— the story of the jerusalem council
a model for interfaith relations?

The voice said to him again, a second time, "What God has made clean, you must not call profane." . . . Then Peter began to speak to them: "I truly understand that God shows no partiality, but in every nation anyone who fears him and does what is right is acceptable to him."

—Acts 10:15, 34, 35

Then certain individuals came down from Judea and were teaching the brothers. "Unless you are circumcised according to the custom of Moses, you cannot be saved." And after Paul and Barnabas had no small dissension and debate with them, Paul and Barnabas and some of the others were appointed to go up to Jerusalem to discuss this question with the apostles and the elders. . . . The apostles and elders met together to consider this matter. . . . The whole assembly kept silence, and listened. . . ."We have decided unanimously to choose representa-

*tives and send them to you, along with our beloved Barnabas and
Paul. . . . For it has seemed good to the Holy Spirit and to us to impose on you
no further burden than these: that you abstain from what has been sacrificed to
idols and from blood and from what is strangled and from fornication. If you
keep yourselves from these, you will do well. Farewell."*

—Acts 15:1-2, 6, 12, 25, 28-29

Preparation

- Read Acts 15: 1-29, the story of the Jerusalem Council.
- In your journal write all of the questions you have about this text as well as your own reflections.
- Spend some time with your questions, letting these questions go deeper and deeper. Note your insights.
- Look at the questions we have asked and write down your thoughts as to where these questions lead you, which may include other questions.
- Spend some time with the text and your journaling before you turn to the reflections that follow.
- After you have read the Reflection section, write down in your journal other insights and questions you have.

Setup

A small round table is in the middle of the room with a circle of chairs around the table, at a comfortable distance. On the table is a single candle as well as symbols from the major religions and a feather. Some light refreshments are in the room. Consider using a feather as a talking piece, a talking piece used in some Native American communities.

Centering

The leader welcomes everyone as the candle is lighted.

Greeting

The leader chooses a greeting that is part of the religious tradition of one of the world religions. The leader invites everyone to stand and introduces the chosen greeting. The leader begins with the person to the left and the greeting flows from each person to the next until it comes back to the leader. One possibility is to use the Hindu greeting of Namaste. In greeting anyone, regardless of faith background, Hindus greet friend and stranger alike with the expression, "Namaste: the God in me greets the God in you." In the greeting, the hands are held together at the palms in front of the heart. The head is bowed slightly.

Hymn
"Let There be Peace on Earth" (**UMH 431**)

Prayer
The "Prayer of St. Francis" — to be prayed in unison.

Lord, make me an instrument of thy peace;
where there is hatred, let me sow love,
where there is injury, pardon;
where there is doubt, faith;
where there is despair, hope;
where there is darkness, light;
and where there is sadness, joy.

O Divine Master,
grant that I may not so much seek
to be consoled as to console;
to be understood, as to understand;
to be loved, as to love;
for it is in giving that we receive,
it is in pardoning that we are pardoned,
and it is in dying that we are born to eternal life.

The leader describes the feather as the usual talking piece in certain Native American circles and then asks if it is acceptable to everyone to use the feather as the talking piece for the discussion of Acts 15 and our relation to people of other faiths. Then the leader asks Circle members to reflect for a moment on their own interfaith relations and to think of a moment in their lives when they saw the image of God in a person of another faith. Passing the talking piece, the leader invites each person to share this moment with the Circle. As always, a person can pass. The talking piece goes around the Circle to the left.

Relational Covenant

The leader reminds everyone of the relational covenant that is posted on the wall. The covenant is read, and everyone affirms his or her commitment to the covenant.

Reading of the Text

Everyone will read together out loud Acts 15:1-29.

Questions

Leader: What follows are just some suggested questions to help you formulate questions for group discussion. We would suggest having four or five questions prepared. Others will flow from the conversation. After each question you ask, use the talking piece passed around the Circle to the left, to hear all of the voices as participants respond to the question. Then hold the talking piece so that the conversation can flow naturally, building on what has been said. When you get to the second question, follow the same practice with the talking piece.

- Why was circumcision and keeping the laws of Moses so important to Jewish Christians?
- What do we learn from the Jerusalem Council about dealing with difficult issues?
- What do we learn from the Jerusalem Council about dealing with those of other faiths?

- What difference does it make in our faith if we understand that Jews and Muslims are children of God created in the image of God?
- When we tell people that they have to be a Christian in order to be saved, how do we compare to the Pharisees who claimed that to be saved you must be circumcised and keep the Law of Moses?

REFLECTION	THE STORY OF THE JERUSALEM COUNCIL—A MODEL FOR INTERFAITH RELATIONS?

These reflections are to stimulate your own thinking, not to limit the possible interpretations and the finding of what is meaningful to you in the passage. In regard to interfaith relations, the focus here is on the Abrahamic religions —Judaism, Christianity and Islam.

HOSTILITY BETWEEN THE JEWS AND THE GENTILES

We know the intensity and the depth of the divisions today between Jews and Muslims in the Middle East. These two communities are having a difficult time living together. In biblical times this hostility was experienced between Gentiles and Jews. D. Smith says, "In Greco-Roman antiquity, the cultural, economic, and political conflict between Jew and Gentile was considered to be the 'prototype' of all human hostility."[105] These two communities were institutionally and historically alienated.[106] We need to appreciate the extent of this hostility in order to understand the change in this relationship begun by Jesus and carried out by his followers. The woman at the well was amazed that Jesus would speak to her. Jesus made the Samaritan the hero of his parable. Jesus was willing to be challenged by the Canaanite woman and extend his healing work beyond the Jewish community, as we learned in Chapter 5. Peter and Paul understood the barrier-breaking spirit of Jesus and began a ministry to the Gentiles.

In Acts we learn that Paul and Barnabas traveled in foreign territories, sharing the good news of Jesus with the Gentiles. They received dramatic responses. They then returned to the sending church in Antioch of Syria. They called the church together to relate "all that God had done with them, and how [God has] opened a door of faith for the Gentiles" (Acts 14:26-27). As one would expect, this movement is met with opposition within the Jewish community. The controversy is expressed at the beginning of Acts 15: "Then certain individuals came down from Judea and were teaching the brothers, 'Unless you are circumcised according to the custom of Moses, you cannot be saved'" (Acts 15:1). In short, you need to become a Jew to become a Christian. The next sentence is probably an understatement, "Paul and Barnabas had no small dissension and debate with them." Paul and Barnabas and some of the others were appointed to go up to Jerusalem to discuss this question with the apostles and the elders (Acts 15:2). This sets the stage for what some call the Jerusalem Council.

Thus begins one of the most remarkable chapters in the Bible, a model for how communities can deal with their differences, break through barriers of hostility, discern God's will, come to a consensus that brings them together and affirms the most important values of all. As we study this scripture together, let us think how the lessons of this chapter might inform how we deal with difficult conversations in the church and also how we might see the overcoming of the hostility between Gentile and Jew as the prototype for our overcoming the hostility between Christians and other religious groups, including Jews and Muslims.[107]

THE COUNCIL

There was "no small dissension and debate" (Acts 15:2). For those who have been involved in church debates around highly important and controversial issues, we have a sense of the emotions that surrounded this debate. Paul and Barnabas, setting an example for all of us, did not shy away from the conflict. They took a long journey from Antioch to Jerusalem to meet with the key leadership of the church to make a communal decision. All participants had the courage to come together to discuss their conflict. They demonstrated how conflict is an opportunity for growth, learning and revelation. The participants in the Jerusalem Council named and defined the conflict. They created the space and time for all voices to be heard, for the stories to be told.

THE ISSUES

The issues discussed are significant to us as Gentiles. We are now included in the covenant as a result of the decisions made at this council. There were two issues, with important underlying interests and needs.

The first issue was circumcision. Did you need to become a Jew to become a Christian? We need to give the folks from Judea their due, as we should in any discussion of a controversial issue. They were sincere human beings. Circumcision was a sign of the covenant. They understood that circumcision was the cornerstone of their understanding of the Law. They were concerned that if circumcision goes, the Law goes. Their deepest interest was preserving the place and importance of the Law. The Law held people together in spite of exile and foreign occupation. The Law gave them the character to resist the culture of idolatry and lack of neighborliness.

The second issue was "social intercourse." Here the focus is on the problem of Jewish and Gentile Christians eating together at the same table, with concern about what is clean and unclean. In some ways, this type of social interaction was a more serious issue because it was at the common meals for Christians that religious fellowship found its deepest expression. Jesus demonstrated the importance and the power of table fellowship.

We believe that no issue we face today is more difficult to resolve than these issues were for the early Christians.

THREE DIFFERENT LENSES

There were many voices at this Council. We wish we knew more about the other voices. We are told of four persons whose three different perspectives were significant to the whole assembly: Peter, Paul and Barnabas, and James.

Peter

Peter notes, "My brothers, you know that in the early days God made a choice among you, that I should be the one through whom the Gentiles would hear the message of the good news and become believers. And God, who knows the human heart, testified to them by giving them the Holy Spirit, just as he did to us; and in cleansing their hearts by faith he has made no distinction between them and us" (Acts 15:7-9).

Peter came to understand his mission to the Gentiles from a vision he received as a result of his encounter with the Roman Centurion, Cornelius, as seen in Acts 10:

> About noon the next day, as they were on their journey and approaching the city, Peter went up on the roof to pray. He became hungry and wanted something to eat, and while it was being prepared, he fell into a trance. He saw the heaven opened and something like a large sheet coming down, being lowered to the ground by its four corners. In it were all kinds of four-footed creatures and reptiles and birds of the air. Then he heard a voice say, "Get up, Peter; kill and eat." But Peter said, "By no means, Lord, for I have never eaten anything that is profane or unclean." The voice said to him again, a second time, "What God has made clean, you must not call profane." This happened three times, and the thing was suddenly taken up to heaven. (Acts 10:9-16)

When Peter met Cornelius, he said to Cornelius and his kin and close friends, "You yourselves know that is unlawful for a Jew to associate with or to visit a Gentile, but God has shown me that I should not call anyone profane or unclean" (Acts 10:28). Peter goes on to see that his vision has far-reaching consequences, "I truly understand that God shows no partiality, but in every nation anyone who fears him and does what is right is acceptable to him" (Acts 10:34-35). This described Cornelius. He feared God and addressed people's needs. This certainly applies to Jews, as he is speaking as a Jew. We know that Christianity began as a Jewish movement. Does Peter's understanding apply to Muslims, who, for example, fear God and do what is right? Think of Muslims in your community who fear God and do what is right.

In Acts 15, Peter notes that God has made "no distinction between them and us" and asks why they need to burden Gentiles with the yoke of observance which Jews themselves had found too heavy to bear. We are "saved through the grace of the Lord Jesus" (Acts 15:7-11). Peter had the courage to stand up and not fear as he did in Antioch, when he backed off from eating with the Gentiles "for fear of the circumcision faction" (Galatians 2:12).

Paul and Barnabas

Paul and Barnabas bear witness to the evident blessing of God on their own mission to the Gentiles. They did not argue. They simply told of the good works of God with the Gentiles (Acts 15:12). This testimony appears to be the most effective of all the approaches. We will speak later of our own experience.

James

James was the brother of Jesus and was a witness to the Resurrection (1 Corinthians 15:7). He was the leader of Jewish Christianity in Jerusalem. Of those who speak, he is the one most identified with Jewish law. It is natural that he looked to scripture for guidance. He quotes from Amos 9:11-12. This scripture expresses the belief that through God's relationship with the Jews all people will come to know God, even the Gentiles. This leads to James' decision that circumcision was not necessary. James says that Peter's relation with Cornelius and other Gentiles is in keeping with scripture. He uses scripture to affirm the new direction, which is contrary to other scripture requiring circumcision.

The Process

"The whole assembly kept silence" (Acts 15:12). They listened deeply. The assembly and the leaders were open to discerning what God was revealing to them. They then came to a consensus, the "consent of the whole church," "unanimously" (Acts 15:22, 25). They came to a decision that what they believed "seemed good to the Holy Spirit" and attempted to address the needs of everyone. There would be no further burden of circumcision, and they recognized the "essentials" of the law, summed up in no food sacrificed to idols (no idolatry) and no fornication (no offenses against neighborliness). The continued observance of abstaining from "whatever has been strangled and from blood" is also a sign of hospitality at table so the Jews and Gentiles could eat together. The Jerusalem Council is a model for holy conferencing in the church. It teaches us the importance of getting together to address our positions, our issues, our problems; having the courage to name them and address the interests and needs of each side; telling and listening to the stories; being open to discern what God is revealing to us through these stories; and affirming that people can come to consensus in a way that meets the important interests and needs of all. Remarkable!

Is the story of the Jerusalem Council a model for interfaith dialogue and reconciliation today?

Practical Importance of the Dialogue

Why is interfaith dialogue so important? Hans Küng says in his book *Global Responsibility*, "No world peace without peace between the religions. No peace between the religions without dialogue between the religions."[108] We are more aware of the truth of these words today than when they were penned in 1991. We know that each of our religions has and can be a source of conflict. As Christians, we know that we all have dark sides to our history, such as the Crusades and the religious wars. We also believe that we all can be a resource for peace. As religious people, in an age of weapons of mass destruction, we cannot allow our religions to be sources of conflict. For the sake of the world, for heaven's sake, we need to discover the resources of peace in our religions and make them our practice.

We don't just discover the need for peace between the world religions on the nightly news. We see it in our own backyards. The fact of the matter is that as our own communities are becoming more diverse we cannot avoid this. Today, for example, there are more Muslims in the United States than either Episcopalians or Presbyterians. According to some reports there are more Muslims than Jews.

We need one another to solve the great issues of our day: poverty, climate change, the threat of weapons of mass destruction, terrorism, just to name a few.

For us, ecumenical discussions have their own excitement, but interfaith dialogues are a lot more challenging and interesting. Everywhere Christians, Muslims and Jews are yearning for bold leadership that is willing to lead and take the risks necessary for building bridges in a deeply divided world.

Theological Imperative for the Dialogue

As Christians, does our faith lead us to engage in dialogue with members of other faiths? To be faithful to God, the creator of this interconnected, interdependent, relational world, who created all in God's own image and who came to reconcile the world, don't we need to engage in interfaith dialogue? We agree with Diana Eck, a United Methodist who teaches at Harvard Divinity School, that "the Gospel is not in the first instance about ideas. It is about relationships that transcend the boundaries of tradition, ethnicity, and social standing. It is even about transgressing the boundaries, restrictions, and legalistic constructs of one's own tradition, just as Jesus did, to reach out to strangers and outsiders." [109] Eck goes on to say that "it is time to stop imagining that God observes the boundaries we set and to think afresh about what Christian faith and commitment really means in a world of many faiths." [110]

To be faithful to the barrier-breaking Jesus — who "broke down the wall of hostility" — don't we need to engage in such dialogue?

To be faithful to the Great Commandment to Love God and Neighbor, don't we need to love our brothers and sisters who are Muslims and Jews? To fulfill the calling to be ministers of reconciliation, don't we need to work toward interfaith reconciliation, which appreciates our differences (God loves differences) and our unity in God?

To obey the commandment not to bear false witness, don't we need to understand one another's religion?

To practice humility, awe and wonder before our God who transcends all of our images and conceptions, don't we need to be open to the truth as found in other religions? Isaiah Berlin said, "It is a terrible and dangerous arrogance to believe that you alone are right, that you have a magical eye which sees the truth and others cannot be right if they disagree. This makes it certain that there is one way, and one only and that it is worth any amount of suffering (particularly on the part of other people) if only the way prevails."[111]

As we have gone deeper into our own faith in Jesus, we have discovered in ourselves an even stronger center in Jesus the Christ who has made our boundaries more porous, more open to the "other." Jesus has led us to the dialogue with the "other," including the religious "other."

THE DIALOGUE

Acts 15 gives us some guidance in this dialogue. We must first have the courage to come together. We need to come together so that we can tell our faith stories and hear the stories of the other. At the heart of such dialogue are stories where we all together share the moments in our lives where we have felt close to God and neighbor. We need to be able to name and address our concerns as well. Most importantly, we need to be open to the Spirit. These dialogues can be a place where we learn and grow and even experience revelation.

OUR EXPERIENCE

Like Paul and Barnabas, our experience has led us to these conversations.

Some of our deepest, richest, most enlightening, fulfilling spiritual experiences have been with people of other religions. Our experience has confirmed that a starting point is practical engagement of the other.

For some of us, our first engagement with someone from a different religious tradition may have been as a child or youth at play. With a smile, I (Tom) recall such a time as a teenager and how future engagement was motivated. I represented the United Christian Youth Movement in Texas at a weeklong camp of 500 Jewish youth, the Temple Teens of Texas. I became the mascot of the largest girl's cabin. I was responsible for the evening prayers, which I was not allowed to recite in person but over the cabin's speaker system. At the Sabbath dinner, I noticed the president greeting campers with a hug and wishing each a "Good Shabbat." I then noticed that all 70 girls of the cabin lined up behind my chair. I had the responsibility of greeting each girl and wishing her a "Good Shabbat." This is when I became truly committed to interfaith dialogue.

At Eastern Mennonite University in their Summer Peacebuilding Institute, I studied with Muslims, Jews, Buddhists and Hindus, among others. Mennonites work quietly all over the world for peace and have gained the respect of people from all religions. In one class, for example, I found myself sitting between a Muslim woman who taught women's studies in Khartoum in the Sudan and a young Muslim woman who organized the women of her area to create a safe zone at the markets and then worked with the elders to bring peace to the tribes of Northern Kenya. When it came to understanding how we are going to live together in this world, we were all on the same page, learning from one another about forgiveness, justice, reconciliation and peace.

My friend, Aziza al-Hibri, a law professor, organized Karamah, Muslim women lawyers for human rights. She invited me to be on their advisory board. These women have taught me what it means to be faithful and courageous. Their piety puts my practices to shame.

You may recall sitting or standing side by side with others at work for your communities and discovering those things in common about which you care deeply. Perhaps it was serving food together in a community soup kitchen, working to stop violence against women and children, providing safe havens for youth at risk in your neighborhood, creating a community garden, hosting a music festival, or being a guest for a sacred meal or ritual in another tradition.

All of these experiences have deepened our own Christian faith.

A VISION

Like Peter, we have experienced what we would call visions. Last year, I (Tom) was invited by friends at Fordham Law School to join 20 law professors and judges to work on "Lawyering and the Love of Neighbor," understanding that the law and lawyers create and define legal relations or obligations, and deal with broken relationships. The group was comprised of Catholics and Protestants, Jews, Muslims and a Buddhist. We worked in a town south of Florence, Italy, created by a Catholic laywomen's movement called Focolare. This movement developed in bomb shelters in 1943 during the bombing of Trent. Chiara Lubich and other women read the Bible and determined that Jesus' prayer in John for unity meant all people, all creation (John 17:21). While we were in Italy, Chiara, the leader of Focolare, died. As we stood around her body, women in their 80s, who were part of the founding of this movement, told us that we were the embodiment of her vision.

SCRIPTURE

Like James, we are informed by scripture. We have already talked about the key scriptures that would guide us in these dialogues. We found them discussed in Chapters 2 and 3 as well as in all of the chapters of this book. Here let's look at the key decision of Acts 15. What if we agreed with Peter, James, Paul and Barnabas, in fact the whole of the Jerusalem Council, that we would emphasize the essentials in our relationships — no idolatry and no lack of neighborliness — loving God and neighbor? Doesn't Peter say the same thing to Cornelius in Acts 10:34-35? "I truly understand that God shows no partiality, but in every nation anyone who fears God and does what is right is acceptable to God."

A CONCLUDING WORD

What happens after the Jerusalem Council we find to be strangely encouraging as well as very human. Paul and Barnabas have just made one of the great breakthroughs in the history of Christianity — overcoming the hostility between Jews and Gentiles in the Christian community. Paul and Barnabas are getting ready "to return and visit the believers in every city" where they proclaimed the word of God. Barnabas wanted to take with them John Mark, but Paul did not want him on the trip as John Mark "had deserted them in Pamphylia and not accompanied them in the work." We are then told, "The disagreement became so sharp that they parted company; Barnabas took Mark with him and sailed away to Cyprus. But in Acts 15:36-41 Paul chose Silas and . . . went through Syria and Cilicia." As far as the record goes, they never reconciled.

This story is an example of what makes the Bible so real and so human. The great victory is described as well as the failure. So Paul and Barnabas are as human as we are. We don't always succeed in our relations, and neither did Paul and Barnabas. We shouldn't give up the journey of forgiveness, restorative justice and reconciliation just because we don't always succeed. In spite of our failures, we need to keep working to live out the call to be ministers of reconciliation as discussed in Chapter 2. Thank God we have a community to encourage us and hold us accountable. Thank God we have been given direction in the Bible. Thank God we have a guide and companion in Jesus. Thank God the Holy Spirit is present in our midst. May we be open to this Spirit. May we strive to live in Peace.

Exercise

• What about having an Abrahamic Family Reunion? Abraham is a significant part of the lineage of Judaism, Christianity and Islam. In Judaism, through Sarah's son Isaac and grandson Jacob, Abraham is the founding

169

patriarch of Israel. God promised Abraham, "I will make of you a great nation, and I will bless you" (Genesis 12:2). With Abraham, God entered into "an everlasting covenant throughout the ages to be God to you and to your offspring after you" (Genesis 17:7). In Islam, Abraham is seen as a prophet and his son Ishmael, whose mother is Hagar, is in the lineage of the prophet Muhammad. Islam considers Abraham to be the "first Muslim" (Surah 3) and the first monotheist. For Christians, Abraham is the father of Israel and a forbear of Christ. We all share in this covenant with Abraham. Is it possible to see ourselves as part of one family tree?

- Let's do some family planning, planning for such a reunion:
    1. In groups of three or four begin thinking about such a reunion.
    2. Who in our community — Jews, Christians and Muslims — should be part of the family planning committee?
    3. How do we first put together this committee?
    4. What kinds of things should we be listening to and learning from others?
    5. What does the invitation look like?
    6. How do we plan for dealing with the conflicts this family has experienced?
    7. Do we need to clear the air before the family gathers with any apologies and or words of forgiveness?
    8. How do we do this in a way that celebrates the uniqueness of each member of the family but also recognizes the unity of the family?
    9. What food should be on the menu, what rituals of greeting and blessing might we use?
    10. Are there songs we should sing and games we want to play?
    11. How do we enable all participants to share their stories?
    12. How do create space for fun and laughter together?
    13. Are there things in our community and world about which we all care deeply?

14. How do we find common goals and a common purpose that will enable us to work together?

15. How do we keep the conversation going?

- After 20 minutes of brainstorming, return to the Circle and share your ideas. Then taking your best ideas, discuss how to actually host such an event at your church or together in a neighboring church.

Closing Ritual

As we conclude our eight sessions together, go around the Circle one last time, asking each person to reflect on the most important lesson learned concerning forgiveness, restorative justice and reconciliation.

Conclude with each person adding a sentence to a concluding prayer that the leader starts and ends with Amen.

Go in Peace!

Notes

105. D. Smith, "The Two Made One: Eph. 2:14-18," *Ohio Journal of Religious Studies*, January 1973, p. 35.

106. Gregory Dix, *Jew and Greek: A Study in the Primitive Church* (Philadelphia: Westminster, 1953).

107. We recognize that there are differences and complexities in biblical scholarship when considering Galatians 2 and Acts 15. We also know that some raise questions concerning the historical accuracy of Acts 15. We are not going to enter those deep waters in this study but focus on the narrative of Acts 15.

108. Hans Küng, *Global Responsibility, In Search of New World Ethic* (New York: Crossroad, 1991), p. xv.

109. Diana L. Eck, "Religious Pluralism, on the Ground and in the Pulpit," *Union Seminary Quarterly Review*, Vol. 56, nos. 3-4 (2002), p. 170.

110. Ibid, p. 178.

111. Isaiah Berlin, "Notes on Prejudice," *The New York Review of Books*, Vol. 48, no. 16 (October 18, 2001), p. 12.

Appendix A
About the South African Truth and Reconciliation Commission

A Different Kind of Justice:
Truth and Reconciliation in South Africa
by Peter Storey

New World Outlook, July-August, 1999
Copyright © 1997 by the *Christian Century*. "A Different Kind of Justice: Truth and Reconciliation in South Africa" by Peter Storey is reprinted by permission from the September 10-17 issue of the *Christian Century*.

The community hall in the dusty township is packed. Most of the people are local Black residents, with a small sprinkling of Whites from the nearby town. On the platform, under South Africa's new flag and a banner proclaiming "Healing Through Truth," the multiracial panel of truth commissioners is listening respectfully.

Facing them, a Black woman speaks of her first-born son who resisted the apartheid regime in the uprising of 1985. She describes his birth and how he was named and speaks proudly of his performance at school.

Then she tells of the night the security police smashed down the door and dragged him away and about how an anonymous policeman sent for her some days later to come to the mortuary. In horrifying detail, she describes the bruised and almost unrecognizable corpse, riddled with 19 bullet wounds, that had been her son.

The remembrance overwhelms her and affects both panel and audience. Some weep quietly while she struggles with her grief. "I do not know if I can forgive," she says. "I must know who did this to my son. When I see the face of the one who killed him, and he tells me why, then perhaps I can forgive."

Arraigned before the judges in another place are three Afrikaners — ex-security police whose vicious rule once ran throughout apartheid South

Africa. One of them reads from a prepared text: "We blindfolded them and took them to a stone quarry outside the town. We hung Subject Number 1 upside down from a tree branch and lit a fire under him. When his hair burned he screamed a lot, then told us everything. The others also confessed. After that, we shot them. Our report said they had resisted arrest."

In the front row are the families of "Subjects 1, 2, and 3." They are learning for the first time how their sons and brothers died. That night the nation also watches and listens to the report on national television.

Hearings like these have been held across the length and breadth of South Africa. The nation's Truth and Reconciliation Commission (TRC) has attracted interest around the world. Its attempt to uncover and deal with a brutal past goes further than any similar exercise in history. Furthermore, the TRC's hearings seem to reach beyond the limitations of secular law, exploring new potentials for forgiveness and national reconciliation. Nowhere else has secular legislation produced such an unsecular and almost scriptural understanding of what it takes to heal a nation.

The Truth Commission's Birth

The birth of the TRC was something of a miracle. By 1990, when then South African President F.W. de Klerk announced negotiations with Nelson Mandela and the African National Congress (ANC), small groups of South Africans — nongovernmental organizations, religious leaders, and human-rights lawyers — had already begun to address the problem of the nation's past. They said there could be no new, united South Africa without a commonly acknowledged history and that this required honestly facing and dealing with the brutal oppression of the apartheid years.

The temptation for the privileged class in South Africa was to believe de Klerk's claim that apartheid was a well-intentioned policy that had failed rather than an intrinsically evil program that had succeeded only too tragically. The majority of Whites refused to acknowledge the systemic nature of the torture, maiming, and assassinations to which individuals had been subjected for more than 30 years by the secret police. In the words of

Archbishop Desmond Tutu: "It's very difficult to wake up someone who is pretending to be asleep."

A further complication was that the political agreement hammered out at the constitutional talks had to be a delicate balance between victory and compromise. Apartheid may have been defeated, but its minions still dominated the police, army, and civil service. Success in the constitutional negotiations depended to a large degree on making a deal with the previous regime. Nuremberg-type trials were not an option if the country was to reach democratic elections without a coup or chaos.

Any successful attempt to address the past would need to both acknowledge the suffering of apartheid's victims and lead to national reconciliation. It had to steer a delicate course between those who cried "prosecute and punish" and those who demanded "forgive and forget." Negotiators created a process that evokes biblical reconciliation, a process that proceeds according to this rubric: "It is necessary to both remember and judge — and forgive."

Selecting the truth commissioners was a challenge. They had to be people of proven integrity and capable of impartiality, with a track record of commitment to human rights and the inner strength to cope with the emotional strain of the job. A balance of race, gender, region, and vocational or professional background was also crucial.

Some 600 nominations were received from the public. A short list of 25 was laid before President Nelson Mandela, who consulted his bipartisan cabinet and made the final cut of 18. He appointed Archbishop Tutu as chair.

Unique TRC Features

The TRC has a number of unique features. First, it gives priority to victims rather than perpetrators. The Gross Human Rights Violations Committee hears the stories of victims across the land. Father Michael Lapsley, half-blinded and maimed by a security police parcel bomb, says that this committee must ensure that people's suffering is "heard, recognized, and reverenced by the nation."

Scores of hearings have been held in city halls and rural community centers. The commission honors the victims by going to them rather than calling them to a central venue. Victims have been empowered by *Khulumani* ("speak-out") groups of fellow victims and have been assisted by hundreds of volunteer statement-takers.

A second unique factor in the work of the TRC is that victims of all sides of the struggle participate. The TRC designers were determined that history would not be sanitized by the victorious side, and so those who suffered at the hands of the liberation forces are also invited to share their experiences. A story of secret police torture may be followed by a White farmer's story of how his wife and children were killed by an ANC landmine or by an account of abuses and torture in one of the liberation movement's training camps. These stories send the important message that a morally justified struggle does not justify indiscriminate killing and deliberate brutality.

The Amnesty Committee, consisting of Supreme Court judges and lawyers, hears pleas for amnesty. The requirements for amnesty are clear. Only individuals — not groups — may apply. There must be full disclosure. The abuses must have been perpetrated to further a political aim. And the principle of "proportionality" must apply. If, for instance, a group of young activists was assassinated by the security police, was it for merely distributing antigovernment pamphlets or for organizing armed resistance? The first case would fail the test of proportionality; the second case might not.

If amnesty is granted, the slate is wiped clean. If not, then disclosures before the commission are not to be used in any subsequent court prosecution. Evidence would have to be independently sought by the attorney general. If the perpetrators didn't come forward by the cut-off date in May 1997, they would live the rest of their lives in fear of being hunted down or fingered by the evidence of a former colleague. As the May 1997 deadline loomed, 8,000 applications flooded in.

A further unique feature of both the Gross Human Rights Violations Committee and the Amnesty Committee is that all their hearings are public. This means that perpetrators have to face the individuals they tortured or the families of those they killed.

Knowing the Truth

A third committee — on Reparations and Rehabilitation — has received less publicity. South Africa's battered economy cannot afford large cash payouts to victims. Other methods of reparation must be fashioned. Thus far, victims' requests have been remarkably modest. Most of all, the bereaved want the return and proper burial of their relatives' remains, or a memorial in their village, or a small scholarship for orphaned children. All agree that the most important thing is to know the truth. Only time will determine the effectiveness of the TRC process. Its stated aims are to produce a record of the violations of the past and make recommendations to prevent them from ever happening again; to acknowledge the suffering of the victims and assist in their rehabilitation; to offer amnesty to past perpetrators; and to facilitate healing and reconciliation for the nation.

Certainly, South Africans are coming nearer to a common view of the recent past. When the emotional victims' hearings began, angry denial was the order of the day. But the cumulative effect of hundreds of accounts of horror and human pain has changed this mood. The sheer volume of similar experiences from every corner of the country, rather than accuracy of detail, has proved the veracity of the stories. What has emerged is a horrific picture of deliberate state terrorism.

Victims do seem to have been helped by telling their stories. Many have said that they now feel able to move forward with their lives. Most important has been the "reverencing" of their suffering. "Today," said an old Black man, "the nation cried my tears with me."

Amnesty, Not Impunity

The issue of amnesty has been more controversial. Some victims' families challenged (unsuccessfully) these provisions in South Africa's highest court. The new constitution guarantees due process and justice for all. Amnesty, they say, denies them that justice. Nevertheless, distasteful as it may be to envisage these brutal state assassins at liberty, most victims seem determined not to become obsessed by their previous tormentors. People are coming to see that even with amnesty, their tormentors are judged — that there is a difference between impunity, implying escape from accountability, and amnesty, which carries profound inward and social consequences.

Some have decried the absence of repentance in many amnesty applications. Apart from the fact that this is a further damning judgment on the distorted morality of these perpetrators, the legislation doesn't require repentance, only the truth. If it did, it would devalue those moments when apparently genuine repentance is volunteered. In one case, a police officer who masterminded the butchering of a number of families in an attack on a rural village faced his victims: "I can never undo what I have done," he said. "I have no right to ask your forgiveness, but I ask that you will allow me to spend my life helping you to rebuild your village and put your lives together." In such moments, anger at the unrepentant is superseded by a glimpse of something more. Out of the horrors of the past, the TRC makes space for grace, and the potential for newness in South Africa shines through.

A Deeper Healing

This potentiality is undoubtedly aided by the person who is chair, Desmond Tutu. He has wept with the victims and marked every moment of repentance and forgiveness with awe. Where a jurist would have been logical, he has not hesitated to be theological. He has sensed when to lead audience members in a hymn to help a victim recover composure and when to call them all to prayer. While some secularists have criticized the God-language he has used, Tutu knows that the nation is seeking a deeper healing than mere law can provide.

Rather than denying justice, the TRC process may be exploring justice in a larger, more magnanimous form — what Charles Villa-Vicencio calls restorative justice as opposed to retributive justice. Perhaps this unique exercise points beyond conventional retribution into a realm where justice and mercy coalesce. It is an area more consistent with Calvary than the courtroom. It is the place where the guilty discover the pain of forgiveness because the innocent are willing to bear the greater pain of forgiving.

Perhaps other nations with wounded histories may find in South Africa a model for hope. As the international community comes to recognize that there is no peace without confronting the hurts of history and without the healing of national and ethnic memories, one nation's attempt to do so may inspire ways in which God could bring newness in these lands too.

Peter Storey is past president of the Methodist Church of South Africa and of the South African Council of Churches. He was a member of the selection committee for the Truth and Reconciliation Commission.

Appendix B
The Nature and Work of Other Truth Commissions

About the Model or Paradigm

Charon Hribar notes in her research about the Truth and Reconciliation Commission (TRC) model that truth-telling is a basic element of the paradigm:

> While the Truth and Reconciliation Commission (TRC) model is always shaped by the particular context in which it is set, there are several basic elements that repeatedly appear in TRC processes that have taken place across the world: (1) they are committed to the task of truth-telling in a process of reconciliation, (2) they are confined to an established time frame, (3) they are charged with an ethical accountability to go beyond mere "fact finding" and to uncover a broader account of past abuses, (4) they are organized in relation to national or international human rights laws, and (5) they are used to put forth particular recommendations that help guide a divided society toward engaging in a process of reconciliation.

Ms. Hribar reminds us that various models of the TRC paradigm have been experienced in nations and communities and the TRC model "emerged in the 20th century to respond to the realities of mass atrocities, political violence, and systemic injustice." In her research, Ms. Hribar offers some insight into the promise and limitations of a truth and reconciliation commission process. More information about this process can be found at the Poverty Initiative, where Ms. Hribar serves as Curriculum Development and Replication Coordinator: http://povertyinitiative.org/tcbackground.

The Work of Truth and Reconciliation Commissions

There are experiences of Truth and Reconciliation Commissions as well as Truth Commissions in nations and communities throughout the world. Some processes are connected to specific political or state mandates. See, for example, The Truth and Reconciliation Commission of Liberia https://www.trcofliberia.org.

Some processes and adaptations of the TRC model are emerging from grassroots and local communities. See, for example: Southern Truth & Reconciliation (S.T.A.R.) http://www.southerntruth.org; Greensboro Truth and Community Reconciliation Project www.gtcrp.org; Poverty Truth Commissions at http://povertyinitiative.org; and Journey Toward the Light Experiences in the Mississippi Annual Conference of the United Methodist Church http://www.mississippi-umc.org.

"The Truth and Reconciliation Commission Model within an On-going Process of Social Transformation"

Research Abstract by Charon Hribar

The Truth and Reconciliation Commission (TRC) model, a justice model designed to investigate human rights violations, is a unique tool that emerged in the 20th century to respond to the realities of mass atrocities, political violence, and systematic injustice. It is a model that has taken varying forms depending on the particular context in which it is implemented, but broadly speaking the TRC has played an important role in publicly confronting the need for those who have been deemed voiceless in the midst of systemic injustice to be heard.

As the model of the TRC continues to attract attention in political, religious and social spheres as a tool to confront structural violence and inequity, it becomes important to reflect on the significance of the TRC model, to think about the lessons that have been learned from past commissions, and to put forth proposals for how such a model might continue to evolve in the future.

Whether talking about mass atrocities that have been committed by oppressive government bodies or the structural abuses of systematic injustices like racism and poverty, the possibility for social restoration and transformation in such contexts requires us to think beyond traditional models of retributive justice.

Aligned with the paradigm of restorative justice and often implemented as a tool of transitional justice in countries emerging from violent conflict, the TRC model has been used as a means to confront past abuses and to seek healing through truth-seeking processes.

While the TRC model emphasizes the importance of truth-telling as a prescript for reconciliation, the time restrictions and documentation objectives often imposed on the official truth commission process can place unintended limitations on the praxis of truth-telling. In an attempt to systematize and affirm the findings of the truth commission, those implementing the TRC model must always be conscience of the making room for the whole truth to be told — meaning truth not restricted to specific events but stories that explore the larger context, history and consequences of human rights violations that have taken place.

As a tool of transformative justice, a justice paradigm closely aligned with restorative justice but that emerges in direct response to long histories of oppression and exploitation, the TRC model should, in the future, be recognized as part of an ongoing process of truth-telling and reconciliation that is working to transform society and the oppressive environments in which human rights violations continue to take place.

The TRC is not a process of forgiving and forgetting but a model where truth-telling can be initiated and legitimized as a step in creating a collective memory that is necessary if social transformation is to take place. Reconciliation cannot begin as long as systems that perpetually oppress members of our human family continue to be maintained.

For the TRC model to be acknowledged as a viable tool for justice making, it must be situated within the paradigm of transformative justice — a paradigm working not to restore a harmony that never existed but to create a new equilibrium where oppression and exploitation are overcome.

This research abstract can now be found at the Truth Commission on Conscience in War. Please visit: http://conscienceinwar.org/category/resources.

Appendix C
How Family and the Future Can Inform Reconciliation

The Power of Grandchildren
By Harriett Jane Olson, Women's Division deputy general secretary

How many women of a "certain age" have you heard say that their grand-children are their Facebook friends, that they follow their grandchildren on Twitter or that they use Skype or some other service to stay in touch? According to the Rev. Gary Mason, mission superintendant at the Method-ist mission in East Belfast, Ireland, thinking about what the world offers their grandchildren has been one of several powerful forces persuading men involved in the militias to get involved and to stay involved in the peace process.

Part of the work of the East Belfast Mission has been to help foster com-munity transformation and renewal in an area of East Belfast that includes Nationalist and Republican communities separated by a "peace wall." The two populations have a fragile point of connection at an "interface," one of the places at which one may pass through the wall.

They are also suffering a common experience of failing schools, lack of economic opportunity and the related health problems. However, what divides them is evident in the wall itself as well as the emotionally loaded flags and murals on display that depict their losses over 40 years of para-military violence. The mission has created a venue for conversation, and many of the flags have been removed. Several of the violent murals have been painted over by scenes from the popular Narnia stories — celebrating C.S. Lewis' Belfast origins.

One of the former paramilitary leaders who has participated in the care-ful and gradual approaches toward reconciliation in East Belfast explained his willingness to participate by saying that he was sobered upon reflecting on the nature of the community that his grandson would inherit. This led him to take the bold step of painting over one of the murals and undergirds his continued participation.

When I visited the mission in June I got to hear several of these men speak about their journeys. They have forged relationships across the traditional dividing lines one careful step at a time from "I'd just as soon shoot him as speak to him" to being able to meet in one another's homes. One shared a story about a phone conversation one day when there had been trouble and the men knew that they had to meet. One of them was recovering from an illness and opened his home to his counterpart. He arrived with grandson in tow. The recovering man shared a home with grandchildren and the men recounted that the children playing together on the back stairs was the "soundtrack" for this important overture. The needs and aspirations of the future were reaching out to sober and realign the present.

The question of where people can gather is a real stumbling block. When all the local territory is either "yours" or "mine" — it is tough work to create an effort that is "ours." Work with women in the community has begun to do so with some shared projects. Work with men in the community is also bringing some small groups together. The plan for the redevelopment of the land on which the mission has been located includes a large central courtyard.

When I looked at the drawings, after having seen the flags and the murals, I said, "Ah, I see, neutral space." Mark Harrison and Sarah Cook of the mission staff explained, "Not neutral space, shared space." Not just space that has had the flags removed or the murals painted over but space that is claimed by the whole community as they branch out in the ways in which they work together. Space that is connected to the education, economic development, psychological health and well-being of the whole community. Space that is needed because the things that bring us together are so much more than the things that drive us apart.

One of those things is our love for our grandchildren and our commitment to a better future for them. Thanks be to God, for the power of grandchildren.

Appendix D
On Restorative Justice

Restorative Justice: The Concept
Movement Sweeping Criminal Justice Field Focuses on
Harm and Responsibility

By Howard Zehr

"A revolution is occurring in criminal justice. A quiet, grassroots, seemingly unobtrusive, but truly revolutionary movement is changing the nature, the very fabric of our work."

These are the opening words in a recent publication of the National Institute of Corrections (NIC) characterizing the combined community and restorative justice movements. Author Eduardo Barajas Jr., a program specialist for NIC, goes on to observe that the changes extend beyond most reforms in the history of criminal justice: "What is occurring now is more than innovative, it is truly inventive . . . a 'paradigm shift.'"

The restorative justice movement has come a long way since probation officer Mark Yantzi and coworker Dave Worth first pushed two shaking offenders toward their victims' homes in Elmira, Ontario, in 1974. Who could have imagined, when we began our version of victim–offender mediation — the Victim Offender Reconciliation Program, or VORP — in Elkhart, Indiana, several years later that we were at the vanguard of a movement with the potential to revolutionize justice?

Crime as Harm
As Barajas' observation implies, restorative justice is not a matter of adding some new programs or tinkering with old ones. Instead, it involves a reorientation of how we think about crime and justice.

At a recent consultation of restorative justice and rehabilitation specialists sponsored by the NIC Academy, participants agreed that two ideas were fundamental: restorative justice is harm-focused, and it promotes the engagement of an enlarged set of stakeholders. Most of restorative justice can be seen as following from these two concepts.

Restorative justice views crime, first of all, as harm done to people and communities. Our legal system, with its focus on rules and laws, often loses sight of this reality; consequently, it makes victims, at best, a secondary concern of justice. A harm focus, however, implies a central concern for victims' needs and roles. Restorative justice begins with a concern for victims and how to meet their needs, for repairing the harm as much as possible, both concretely and symbolically.

A focus on harm also implies an emphasis on offender accountability and responsibility — in concrete, not abstract, terms. Too often we have thought of accountability as punishment, as pain administered to offenders for the pain they have caused. Unfortunately, this often is irrelevant or even counterproductive to real accountability. Little in the justice process encourages offenders to understand the consequences of their actions or to empathize with victims. On the contrary, the adversarial game requires offenders to look out for themselves. Offenders are discouraged from acknowledging their responsibility and are given little opportunity to act on this responsibility in concrete ways. The "neutralizing strategies" — the stereotypes and rationalizations that offenders use to distance themselves from the people they hurt — are never challenged. So the sense of alienation from society experienced by many offenders, the feeling that they themselves are victims, is only heightened by the legal process and the prison experience.

If crime is essentially about harm, accountability means being encouraged to understand that harm, to begin to comprehend the consequences of one's behavior. Moreover, it means taking responsibility to make things right insofar as possible, both concretely and symbolically. As our foreparents knew well, wrong creates obligations; taking responsibility for those obligations is the beginning of genuine accountability.

The principle of engagement suggests that the primary parties affected by crime victims — offenders, members of the community — are given significant roles in the justice process. Indeed, they need to be given information about one another and to be involved in deciding what justice requires in this situation. In some cases, this may mean actual dialogue between these parties, as happens in victim/offender mediation or family group conferences, to come to a consensus about what should be done. In others, it may involve indirect exchange or the use of surrogates. In any eventuality, the principle of engagement implies involvement of an enlarged circle of parties as compared to the traditional justice process.

At the risk of oversimplifying, the restorative justice and the traditional justice approach — retributive justice — might be summarized as follows:

Retributive Justice

Crime	is a violation of the law, and the state is the victim.
The aim of justice	is to establish blame (guilt) and administer pain (punishment).
The process of justice	is a conflict between adversaries in which the offender is pitted against state rules, intentions outweigh outcomes and one side wins while the other loses.

Restorative Justice

Crime	is a violation or harm to people and relationships.
The aim of justice	is to identify obligations, to meet needs and to promote healing.
The process of justice	involves victims, offenders and the community in an effort to identify obligations and solutions, maximizing the exchange of information (dialogue, mutual agreement) between them.

To put restorative justice in its simplest form: crime violates people and violations create obligations. Justice should involve victims, offenders and community members in a search to identify needs and obligations so as to promote healing among the parties involved.

Widespread Interest

Today's interest in restorative justice at the national level follows several decades of innovation and experimentation at the community and state levels. Victim/offender mediation programs have sprung up in at least 300 U.S. and Canadian communities. The Minnesota Department of Corrections has on staff a restorative justice planner who is working innovatively to help communities in that state develop new restorative approaches. Vermont has rethought the concept of probation, designing a "reparative probation" system for nonviolent offenders. Native American and Canadian communities are finding ways to put into operation some of their traditional approaches and values; these approaches also are being seen as part of a restorative justice framework. In academic and consulting fields, too, numerous restorative justice institutes and programs are emerging.

This interest in restorative justice is not limited to North America. Hundreds of victim/offender mediation programs have developed in European countries; Germany, Finland and England, for example, have many such programs. South Africa is writing a new juvenile justice code incorporating restorative principles. In New Zealand, restorative justice has served to guide and help shape the family group conference approach, which is now the basis of that country's entire juvenile justice system.

Deciphering Terms

"Restorative justice" is a term that quickly connects for many people, and therein lies both its strength and its weakness. Many professionals as well as laypeople are frustrated with justice as it is commonly practiced and are immediately attracted to the idea of restoration. Restorative justice intuitively suggests a reparative, person-centered, commonsense approach. For many of us, it reflects values with which we were raised. As a result, the term has been widely embraced and used in many contexts.

But what do we mean by "restorative justice?" Will the term be used simply as a new way to name and justify the same old programs and goals? Many programs can be compatible with restorative justice if they are reshaped to fully account for restorative principles. If they are not reshaped as part of a larger restorative "lens," however, at best they will be more of the same. At worst, they may become new ways to control and punish.

All of this is not to say that there is such a thing as "pure" restorative or retributive justice. Rather, justice should be seen as a continuum between two ideal types. On the one end is our Western legal system. Its strengths — such as the encouragement of human rights — are substantial. Yet it has important weaknesses. Criminal justice tends to be punitive, conflictual, impersonal and state-centered. It encourages the denial of responsibility and empathy on the part of offenders. It leaves victims out, ignoring their needs. Instead of discouraging wrongdoing, it often encourages it. It exacerbates rather than heals wounds.

At the other end is the restorative alternative. Victims' needs and rights are central, not peripheral. Offenders are encouraged to understand the harm they have caused and to take responsibility for it. Dialogue — direct or indirect — is encouraged, and communities play important roles. Restorative justice assumes that justice can and should promote healing, both individual and societal.

Criminal justice usually is not purely retributive. On the other hand, we rarely will achieve justice that is fully restorative. A realistic goal is to move as far as we can toward a process that puts victims, offenders and members of the affected community — and their respective needs and roles — at the center of our search for a justice that heals.

Bibliography

LIS Inc. Community Justice: Striving for Safe, Secure and Just Communities. Aurora, Colo.: National Institute of Corrections, March 1996.
Howard Zehr is professor of sociology and restorative justice at Eastern Mennonite University and director of the Mennonite Central Committee U.S. Office on Crime and Justice. Copies of the "restorative justice signposts" bookmark (and a list of other criminal justice resources) are available without charge from Literature Resources, Mennonite Central Committee, 21 S. 12th. Akron, PA 17501; (717) 859-1151; e-mail: see@mcc.org.

RESTORATIVE JUSTICE SIGNPOSTS

We are working toward restorative justice when we . . .

I. Focus on the harms of wrongdoing more than the rules that have been broken

II. Show equal concern and commitment to victims and offenders, involving both in the process of justice

III. Work toward the restoration of victims, empowering them and responding to their needs as they see them

IV. Support offenders while encouraging them to understand, accept and carry out their obligations

V. Recognize that while obligations may be difficult for offenders, they should not be intended as harms, and they must be achievable

VI. Provide opportunities for dialogue, direct or indirect, between victims and offenders as appropriate

VII. Involve and empower the affected community through the justice process and increase its capacity to recognize and respond to community bases of crime

VIII. Encourage collaboration and reintegration rather than coercion and isolation

IX. Give attention to the unintended consequences of our actions and programs

X. Show respect to all parties, including victims, offenders and justice colleagues

—Harry Mika and Howard Zehr

	RETRIBUTIVE JUSTICE	RESTORATIVE JUSTICE
PROBLEM	defined narrowly, abstractly, a legal infraction only legal variables relevant state as victim	defined relationally, as a violation of people overall context relevant people as victims
ACTORS	state (active) and offender (passive)	victim and offender primary, along with community and state
PROCESS	adversarial, authoritarian, technical, impersonal focus = guilt/blame "neutralizing strategies" encouraged	participatory, maximizing information, dialogue and mutual agreement focus = needs and obligations empathy and responsibility encouraged
OUTCOME	pain, suffering harm by offender balanced by harm to offender oriented to past	making things right by identifying needs and obligations, healing, problem solving harm by offender balanced by making right oriented to future

Appendix E
Hymn

Walls Mark Our Bound'ries

Words by Ruth C. Duck, 1994

Music: PENROSE, by Jim Strathdee, 1996

"Walls Mark Our Bound'ries," in *Circles of Care: Hymns and Songs*, by Ruth C. Duck and Jim Strathdee (Cleveland: The Pilgrim Press, 1998). Words and Music © The Pilgrim Press. All rights reserved. Used by permission.

Note: This hymn is included for use in Chapter 5.

Chorus

So build us a ta-ble and tear down the wall!

Christ is our host. There is room_____

_____ for us all!

all!_____

Appendix F
For Further Reading

Introduction

Boyes-Watson, Carolyn. *Peacemaking Circles and Urban Youth, Bringing Justice Home*. St. Paul: Living Justice Press, 2008.

McFee, Marcia. "Ritual Formation: Liturgical Practices and the Practice of Peacebuilding," in *Conflict and Communion, Reconciliation and Restorative Justice at Christ's Table*, ed. Thomas Porter. Nashville: Discipleship Resources, 2006.

Porter, Thomas. *The Spirit and Art of Conflict Transformation, Creating a Culture of JustPeace*. Nashville: Upper Room Books, 2010.

Pranis, Kay. *The Little Book of Circle Processes*. Intercourse, Pa.: Good Books, 2005.

Wheatley, Margaret J. *Turning to One Another: Simple Conversations to Restore Hope to the Future*. San Francisco: Berrett-Koehler Publishers, Inc., 2002.

Wink, Walter. *The Bible in Human Transformation*. Philadelphia: Fortress Press, 1973.

Wink, Walter. *Transforming Bible Study: A Leader's Guide*. Nashville: Abingdon Press, 1980.

Chapter 1

Brueggemann, Walter. *Genesis: Interpretation: A Bible Commentary for Teaching and Preaching*. Atlanta: John Knox, 1982.

Fiditch, Susan. "Genesis," in *The Women's Bible Commentary*, eds. Carol Newsom and Sharon H. Ringe. Louisville: Westminster John Knox Press, 1992.

Hixon, Stephanie Anna and Porter, Thomas W., Jr. "The Real Life Journey of Rebecca's Son, Jacob," in *United Methodist Women 2011 Program Book* "Finding Peace," Delgado, Sharon, et al. New York: The Women's Division, General Board of Global Ministries, The United Methodist Church, 2010.

Chapter 2

Battle, Michael. *Reconciliation: The Ubuntu Theology of Desmond Tutu*. Cleveland: The Pilgrim Press, 1997.

Brueggemann, Walter. "Vision for a New Church and a New Century, Part 2: Holiness Become Generosity." Lecture. *Union Seminary Quarterly Review*, Vol. 54 (2000), pp. 21-39.

Lederach, John Paul. *The Journey Toward Reconciliation*. Scottdale, Pa.: Herald Press, 1999.

Schreiter, Robert. *Reconciliation: Mission and Ministry in a Changing Social Order*. Maryknoll, N.Y.: Boston Theological Institute, Cambridge, Massachusetts, 1997.

Chapter 3

Enns, Elaine and Myers, Ched. *Ambassadors of Reconciliation*, Vol. I. New York: Orbis Books, 2009.

Swartley, Willard M. *Covenant of Peace: The Missing Peace in New Testament Theology and Ethics*. Cambridge, U.K.: William B. Eerdmans Publishing Co., 2006.

Chapter 4

Botcharova, Olga. "Implementation of Track Two Diplomacy: Developing a Model of Forgiveness," in *Forgiveness and Reconciliation: Religion, Public Policy and Conflict Transformation*, eds. Raymond Helmick and Rodney Petersen. Philadelphia: Templeton Press, 2002.

Herman, Judith. *Trauma and Recovery: The Aftermath — From Domestic Abuse to Political Terror*. New York: Basic Books, 1992.

O'Day, Gail R. "John," in *The Women's Bible Commentary*, eds. Carol Newsom and Sharon H. Ringe. Louisville: Westminster John Knox Press, 1992 (see also the Expanded Edition, Presbyterian Publishing Corporation, 1998).

Yoder, Carolyn. *The Little Book of Trauma Healing*. Intercourse, Pa.: Good Books, 2005.

Chapter 5

Lederach, John Paul. *The Moral Imagination, The Art and Soul of Building Peace*. London: Oxford University Press, 2005.

Porter, Thomas, ed., *Conflict and Communion, Reconciliation and Restorative Justice at Christ's Table*. Nashville: Discipleship Resources, 2006.

Chapter 6

Jones, L. Gregory. *Embodying Forgiveness: A Theological Analysis*. Grand Rapids: Wm. B. Eerdmans Publishing Co., 1995.

Tutu, Desmond Mpilo. *No Future Without Forgiveness*. New York: Image, Doubleday, 1999.

Volf, Miroslav. *Exclusion and Embrace: A Theological Exploration of Identity, Otherness, and Reconciliation*. Nashville: Abingdon Press, 1996.

Chapter 7

De Gruchy, John W. *Reconciliation: Restoring Justice*. Minneapolis: Augsburg Fortress Publishers, 2003.

Marshall, Christopher. *Beyond Retribution: A New Testament Vision for Justice, Crime and Punishment*. Grand Rapids: Wm. B. Eerdmans Publishing Co., 2001.

Ross, Rupert. *Returning to the Teachings*. Toronto, Ontario: Penguin, 1996.

Wray, Harmon L. and Peggy Hutchison. *Restorative Justice: Moving Beyond Punishment,* with *Study Guide* by Brenda Connelly. New York: General Board of Global Ministries, The United Methodist Church, 2002.

Zehr, Howard. *The Little Book of Restorative Justice*. Intercourse, Pa.: Good Books, 2002.

Chapter 8

Eck, Diana L. "Religious Pluralism, on the Ground and in the Pulpit." *Union Seminary Quarterly Review*, Vol. 56, nos. 3-4 (2003), p. 170.

LeBaron, Michelle and Venashri Pillay. *Conflict Across Cultures: Unique Experience of Bridging Differences*. Boston: Intercultural Press, Nicholas Brealey Publishing, 2006.

Sacks, Jonathan. *Dignity of Difference: How to Avoid the Clash of Civilizations*. New York: Continuum International Publishing Group, 2003.

Speight, Marston. *Creating Interfaith Communities,* with *Study Guide* by Glory and Jacob Dharmaraj. New York: General Board of Global Ministries, The United Methodist Church, 2003.

http://www.overcomingviolence.org

Additional Exploration

Battle, Michael. *Reconciliation: The Ubuntu Theology of Desmond Tutu*. Cleveland: The Pilgrim Press, 1997.

Botcharova, Olga. "Implementation of Track Two Diplomacy: Developing a Model of Forgiveness," in *Forgiveness and Reconciliation: Religion, Public Policy and Conflict Transformation*, eds. Raymond Helmick and Rodney Petersen. Philadelphia: Templeton Press, 2002.

Boyes-Watson, Carolyn. *Peacemaking Circles and Urban Youth, Bringing Justice Home*. St. Paul: Living Justice Press, 2008.

Brueggemann, Walter. *Genesis: Interpretation: A Bible Commentary for Teaching and Preaching*. Atlanta: John Knox Press, 1982.

Brueggemann, Walter. "Vision for a New Church and a New Century, Part 2: Holiness Become Generosity." *Lecture, Union Seminary Quarterly Review*, Vol. 54, (2000).

De Gruchy, John W. Reconciliation: *Restoring Justice*. Minneapolis: Augsburg Fortress Publishers, 2003.

Eck, Diana L. "Religious Pluralism, on the Ground and in the Pulpit." *Union Seminary Quarterly Review*, Vol. 56, nos. 3-4 (2002), p. 170.

Enns, Elaine and Ched Myers. *Ambassadors of Reconciliation*, Volume I. New York: Orbis Books, 2009.

Herman, Judith. *Trauma and Recovery: The Aftermath — From Domestic Abuse to Political Terror*. New York: Basic Books, 1992.

Jones, L. Gregory. *Embodying Forgiveness: A Theological Analysis*. Grand Rapids: Wm. B. Eerdmans Publishing Co., 1995.

LeBaron, Michelle and Venashri Pillay. *Conflict Across Cultures: Unique Experience of Bridging Differences*. Boston: Intercultural Press, Nicholas Brealey Publishing, 2006.

Lederach, John Paul. *The Journey Toward Reconciliation*. Scottdale, Pa.: Herald Press, 1999.

Lederach, John Paul. *The Moral Imagination, The Art and Soul of Building Peace*. London: Oxford University Press, 2005.

Marshall, Christopher. *Beyond Retribution: A New Testament Vision for Justice, Crime and Punishment*. Grand Rapids: Wm. B. Eerdmans Publishing Co., 2001.

McFee, Marcia. "Ritual Formation: Liturgical Practices and the Practice of Peace-building," in C*onflict and Communion, Reconciliation and Restorative Justice at Christ's Table*, ed. Thomas Porter. Nashville: Discipleship Resources, 2006.

Newsom, Carol and Ringe, Sharon H. eds. *The Women's Bible Commentary*. Louisville: Westminster John Knox Press, 1992 (see also the Expanded Edition, Presbyterian Publishing Corporation, 1998).

Porter, Thomas, ed. *Conflict and Communion, Reconciliation and Restorative Justice at Christ's Table*. Nashville: Discipleship Resources, 2006.

Porter, Thomas. *The Spirit and Art of Conflict Transformation, Creating a Culture of JustPeace*. Nashville: Upper Room Books, 2010.

Pranis, Kay. *The Little Book of Circle Process*. Intercourse, Pa.: Good Books, 2005.

Rambo, Shelly. *Spirit and Trauma: A Theology of Remaining*. Louisville: Westminster John Knox Press, 2010.

Ross, Rupert. *Returning to the Teachings.* Toronto, Ontario: Penguin, 1996.

Sacks, Jonathan. *Dignity of Difference: How to Avoid the Clash of Civilizations.* New York: Continuum International Publishing Group, 2003.

Schreiter, Robert. *Reconciliation: Mission and Ministry in a Changing Social Order.* Maryknoll, N.Y.: Boston Theological Institute, Cambridge, Massachusetts, 1997.

Speight, Marston. *Creating Interfaith Communities,* with *Study Guide* by Glory and Jacob Dharmaraj. New York: General Board of Global Ministries, The United Methodist Church, 2003.

Swartley, Willard M. *Covenant of Peace: The Missing Peace in New Testament Theology and Ethics.* Cambridge, U.K.: William B. Eerdmans Publishing Co., 2006.

Tutu, Desmond Mpilo. *No Future Without Forgiveness.* New York: Image, Doubleday, 1999.

Volf, Miroslav. *Exclusion and Embrace: A Theological Exploration of Identity, Otherness, and Reconciliation.* Nashville: Abingdon Press, 1996.

Wheatley, Margaret J. *Turning to One Another: Simple Conversations to Restore Hope to the Future.* San Francisco: Berrett-Koehler Publishers, Inc., 2002.

Wink, Walter. *The Bible in Human Transformation.* Philadelphia: Fortress Press, 1973.

Wink, Walter. *The Powers That Be: Theology for a New Millennium.* New York: Doubleday, 1998.

Wink, Walter. *Transforming Bible Study: A Leader's Guide.* Nashville: Abingdon Press, 1980.

Wray, Harmon L. and Peggy Hutchison. *Restorative Justice: Moving Beyond Punishment,* with *Study Guide* by Brenda Connelly. New York: General Board of Global Ministries, The United Methodist Church, 2002.

Yoder, Carolyn. *The Little Book of Trauma Healing.* Intercourse, Pa.: Good Books, 2005.

Zehr, Howard. *The Little Book of Restorative Justice.* Intercourse, Pa.: Good Books, 2002.

http://www.overcomingviolence.org.

ABOUT THE AUTHORS

Stephanie Anna Hixon

With the hope of providing services that support wholeness and well-being for individuals, communities and
institutional systems, Stephanie Hixon seeks to integrate
best practices in alternative dispute resolution with principles of faith and spirituality, communication theory
and creative organic group processes.

Earning degrees in music therapy and music education from Shenandoah College and Conservatory of Music (Shenandoah University), she later
pursued theological coursework through the Washington, D.C., consor-
tium of schools, earning a master of divinity degree from Lutheran Theological Seminary at Gettysburg. Her professional certification in alternative
dispute resolution was granted by Hamline University School of Law. She
is an ordained elder in the Susquehanna Annual Conference of the United
Methodist Church and served congregations in Pennsylvania and West
Virginia. Stephanie also served as a member of the general secretariat for
the General Commission on the Status and Role of Women in the United
Methodist Church, providing leadership as an advocate for a diverse con-
stituency of women within the Church. During her tenure as general secretary she offered expertise and support for the Church's response to sexual
harassment, abuse and misconduct.

Stephanie is a trained consultant and facilitator in severely conflicted
situations and has extensive experience with strategies and processes to assist institutions and communities to foster environments of mutual respect
and regard for all persons. Serving as co-executive director for JustPeace
Center for Mediation and Conflict Transformation in the United Methodist Church provides an opportunity for Stephanie to embrace her passion
for justice, peacemaking and conflict transformation. In addition to training, teaching and consulting, she has facilitated mediations and circles of
accountability and healing within the Church. Along with her colleague

Tom Porter, she believes that local churches can be centers of relational healing and peace building for their members as well as the neighborhoods in which they reside.

Thomas Porter

Tom Porter is a United Methodist minister, teacher, mediator and trial lawyer. He is co-executive director of JustPeace Center for Mediation and Conflict Transformation, the United Methodist Church. He is also co-executive director of the Religion and Conflict Transformation Program at Boston University School of Theology. After graduating from Yale University, he received a master of divinity degree from Union Theological Seminary and a Juris Doctor from Boston University Law School. He studied mediation at Harvard Law School and Eastern Mennonite University.

Tom is an ordained elder of the New England Conference of the United Methodist Church. For 23 years, Tom was the chancellor for this conference. He was a founding partner of the trial firm of Melick & Porter LLP in 1983 and has been a trial lawyer since 1974, representing religious institutions, universities, hospitals, professionals, nonprofit organizations and others. He is a member of the board of the *Journal of Law and Religion* and was chair of the board from 1989 through 2001. He was a founder and the president of the Council of Religion and Law, a society of law professors and theologians as well as lawyers and ministers, from 1978 to 1985.

He served on the board of Union Theological Seminary, chairing its educational policy committee, from 1992 to 2001. He has taught at various schools, including Union Theological Seminary in New York City, Claremont School of Theology, the Theological School of Drew University, Iliff School of Theology and Pepperdine Law School. Currently, he is a lecturer at Boston University School of Theology. He is the author of *The Spirit and Art of Conflict Transformation: Creating a Culture of JustPeace* and the editor of *Conflict and Communion: Reconciliation and Restorative Justice at Christ's Table*. He is now writing a book on the theology and jurisprudence of restorative justice.

ADDITIONAL RESOURCES

Un Camino a Recorrer
Perdón, Justicia Restauradora y Reconciliación
Stephanie Hixon y Thomas Porter
The Journey: Forgiveness, Restorative Justice and Reconciliation
(Spanish translation)
M3111-2011-01
$7.00

여정
용서, 정의의 회복 그리고 화해
스테파니 힉슨, 토마스 포터
(Korean translation)
M3112-2011-01
$7.00

Spiritual Growth Youth Study, Forgiveness and Reconciliation
Jenny Youngman
M3113-2011-01
$8.00

Available from: Mission Resource Center

800-305-9857

www.missionresourcecenter.org

or

www.unitedmethodistwomen.org/thejourney

Personal Notes